REGULATION OF U.S. EQUITY MARKETS

REGULATION OF U.S. EQUITY MARKETS

edited by

Robert A. Schwartz
Baruch College, CUNY, U.S.A.

assisted by

Antoinette Colaninno

KLUWER ACADEMIC PUBLISHERS
Boston / Dordrecht / London

Distributors for North, Central and South America:
Kluwer Academic Publishers
101 Philip Drive
Assinippi Park
Norwell, Massachusetts 02061 USA
Telephone (781) 871-6600
Fax (781) 681-9045
E-Mail <kluwer@wkap.com>

Distributors for all other countries:
Kluwer Academic Publishers Group
Distribution Centre
Post Office Box 322
3300 AH Dordrecht, THE NETHERLANDS
Telephone 31 78 6392 392
Fax 31 78 6546 474
E-Mail <services@wkap.nl>

Electronic Services <http://www.wkap.nl>

Library of Congress Cataloging-in-Publication Data

Regulation of U.S. equity markets / edited by Robert A. Schwartz ; assisted by Antoinette Colaninno.
p.cm.
Proceedings of a conference held at the Zicklin School of Business March 17, 1999.
Includes bibliographical references and index.
ISBN 0-7923-7282-4 (alk.paper)
1.Stock exchanges--Law and legislation--United States. 2. Securities industry--Law and legislation--United States. I. Title: Regulation of United States equity markets. II. Schwartz, Robert A. (Robert Alan), 1937 - III. Colaninno, Antoinette.

KF1070.A2 R44 2001
346.73'0926--dc21 2001046203

Printed on acid-free paper.
Printed in the United States of America

Contents

List of Participants

Keynote Speakers

Alfred R. Berkeley, III*	Vice Chairman	The Nasdaq Stock Market, Inc.

* At the time of the conference, Alfred Berkeley was President, The Nasdaq Stock Market, Inc.

William R. Johnston	President and COO	New York Stock Exchange
Richard F. Syron*	Chairman and CEO	Thermo Electron Corporation

*At the time of the conference, Richard Syron was Chairman and CEO of the American Stock Exchange.

Laura S. Unger*	Acting Chairman	U.S. Securities and Exchange Commission

* At the time of the conference, Laura Unger was Commissioner, U.S. Securities and Exchange Commission

Panelists

Alden S. Adkins	Senior Vice President and General Counsel	NASD Regulation, Inc.
Matthew Andresen	President	Island ECN
James J. Angel	Associate Professor of Finance	Georgetown University
Douglas M. Atkin	President and CEO	Instinet Corporation
Frank E. Baxter	Chairman	Jefferies & Company, Inc.
Brandon Becker	Partner	Wilmer, Cutler & Pickering
Robert Colby	Deputy Director, Division of Market Regulation	U.S. Securities and Exchange Commission
Mike Cormack*	President	Archipelago

*At the time of the conference, Mike Cormack was Manager of Equity Trading at American Century Investment Management.

Paul Davis	Senior Managing Director	TIAA-CREF

Ian Domowitz	Smeal Professor of Finance	Pennsylvania State University
Kevin M. Foley	President	Bloomberg Tradebook
E.E. (Buzzy) Geduld	President and CEO	Herzog Heine Geduld
William R. Harts	Managing Director, Global Direct Equity Markets Group	Salomon Smith Barney
Raymond L. Killian, Jr.	Chairman, President and CEO	Investment Technology Group
Edward A. Kwalwasser	Group Executive Vice President	New York Stock Exchange
Ruben Lee	Director	Oxford Finance Group
William A. Lupien	Chairman	OptiMark, Inc.

*At the time of the conference, Bill Lupien was Chairman and CEO of OptiMark Technologies.

Peter B. Madoff	Senior Managing Director	Bernard L. Madoff Investment Securities
Mike Murphy	Managing Director of Equity Trading	First Union Securities
Jeanne L. Murtaugh	Vice Chairman	BNY ESI & Company
Maureen O'Hara	Purcell Professor of Finance	Cornell University
Arthur J. Pacheco*	Senior Managing Director	Bear Stearns & Company

*At the time of the conference, Arthur Pacheco was President and CEO of Strike Technologies.

Aldo Parcesepe	Senior Manager	Bear Stearns & Company
Ernest T. Patrikis	Special Advisor to the Chairman	American International Group
Junius W. Peake	Monfort Distinguished Professor of Finance	University of Northern Colorado
Gerald Putnam	Founder and CEO	Archipelago
Evan Schulman*	Co-Founder	Upstream Technologies

*At the time of the conference, Evan Schulman was Co-Founder of Lattice Trading, which was acquired by State Street Bank.

Robert A. Schwartz	Speiser Professor of Finance and University Distinguished Professor	Baruch College
Erik R. Sirri*	Assistant Professor	Babson College

At the time of the conference, Erik Sirri was Chief Economist at the U.S. Securities and Exchange Commission.

Benn Steil	Senior Fellow and Linda J. Wachner Chair in Foreign Economic Policy	Council on Foreign Relations
Hans R. Stoll	Walker Professor of Finance and Director of the Financial Markets Research Center	Vanderbilt University

Richard Sylla	Kaufman Professor of The History of Financial Institutions and Markets	New York University
Daniel G. Weaver	Associate Professor of Finance	Baruch College
Robert A. Wood	Distinguished Professor of Finance	University of Memphis
John C. Woodman	Managing Director	UBS Warburg
R. Steven Wunsch	President and CEO	AZX, Inc.

Participants from the Floor

Timothy Baikie*	Director, Global Market Initiatives	Toronto Stock Exchange

*At the time of the conference, Timothy Baikie was Special Counsel, Market Regulation, at the Toronto Stock Exchange.

Allan Grody	President	Financial InterGroup
Diana Henriques	Reporter	New York Times
Greg Ip	Reporter	Wall Street Journal
Holly Stark*	Director of Trading	Kern Capital Management

*At the time of the conference, Holly Stark was a trader at Dalton, Greiner, Hartman, Maher.

Donald E. Weeden*	Manager	Clearwater Ventures and WEB Investors

* Mr. Weeden is also Chairman of Weeden Securities Corporation, the General Partner of Weeden & Company.

Conference Sponsors

American Stock Exchange
Bloomberg Tradebook
Herzog, Heine, Geduld, Inc.
Instinet Corporation
Investment Technology Group, Inc.
Jefferies & Company, Inc.
The Nasdaq Stock Market, Inc.
New York Stock Exchange
Bernard L. Madoff Investment Securities
OptiMark Technologies, Inc.
Security Traders Association
State Street Corporation
Terra Nova

Preface

This book contains the proceedings of a one-day conference, *Regulation of the U.S. Equity Markets,* held at the Zicklin School of Business on March 17, 1999. Included are the edited transcripts of the panel discussions and of four addresses by: William R. Johnston, President and COO of the New York Stock Exchange; Richard F. Syron, who at the time was Chairman and CEO of the American Stock Exchange; Alfred R. Berkeley, President of the Nasdaq Stock Market; and Laura S. Unger, Commissioner of the U.S. Securities and Exchange Commission.

In the past quarter of a century, the pace of structural change in the equity markets has accelerated dramatically and, as it has, regulation has come to play an increasingly central role in the development of market structure. The purpose of this book is to consider regulation's contribution to the efficiency of the U.S. equity markets. Sharply different opinions are expressed on the matter, as the discussion ranges from congressional oversight, to SEC involvement in market structure issues, to the self-regulatory responsibilities of the market centers – most notably, the New York Stock Exchange and the Nasdaq Stock Market.

It is not surprising that the equity markets have come under the scrutiny of the regulators. Their size and significance to the economic health of the country make them critically important and highly visible. The tendency of order flow to concentrate in major market centers raises the fear of monopolistic power, even as the dispersion of order flow across alternative markets raises fears of fragmentation. Externalities exist in trading (e.g., my limit order gives you a free option to trade) and market making has public goods characteristics (e.g., greater liquidity provides better price discovery for the broad market). The vested interests of intermediaries and people's reluctance to learn a new technology cause technological inertia. And so forth.

In discussions concerning market structure, it is helpful to recognize that market centers produce two things: trades and information. The first, the transfer of shares from sellers to buyers, is the easier of the two. The second, which involves the determination of quotes and prices, is complicated. The SEC has rightly been concerned about the production and distribution of information. This focus is clear from two SEC releases that were issued after the Zicklin conference. In the first, "Regulation of Market Information Fees" (Release No. 34-42208; File No. S7-28-99), the Commission emphasized that retail investors must have access to market information, that information must be consolidated, that transparency must be enhanced, and that the SEC must be proactively involved:

- One of the most important functions that the Commission can perform for retail investors is to ensure that they have access to the information they need to protect and further their own interests (page 7).
- Although it intended to rely on competitive forces to the greatest extent possible to shape the national market system, Congress also recognized that the Commission would need ample authority to achieve the goal of providing investors and broker-dealers with a central source of consolidated market information (page 33).
- The consolidated, real-time stream of market information has been an essential element in the success of the U.S. securities markets. It is the principal tool for enhancing the transparency of the buying and selling interest in a security, for addressing the fragmentation of buying and selling interest among different market centers, and for facilitating the best execution of customers' orders by their broker-dealers. Broad public access to consolidated market information was not the fortuitous result of private market forces, but of planning and concerted effort by Congress, the Commission, the SROs, and the securities industry as a whole (page 5).

In the second SEC release, "Market Fragmentation" (Release No. 34-42450; file No. SR-NYSE-99-48), the Commission added the thought that limit orders and quotes may be isolated from full interaction and that price competition may be insufficient:

- The Commission is concerned, however, that customer limit orders and dealer quotes may be isolated from full interaction with other buying and selling interest in today's markets (page 3).
- ...a market structure that provides a full and fair opportunity for interaction of investor trading interest may, by enhancing price competition, reduce the transaction costs of investors who submit market orders (page 9).

But the SEC cannot be involved in the production, distribution and pricing of information without interfering with the natural formation of a marketplace, and a commonly expressed fear is that regulatory intervention can have consequences that are difficult to predict and very hard to control. Also questioned is how nimble a governmental authority would be in repairing a mistake if a market structure innovation that it has brought about does not work. Consequently, the current level of regulatory involvement in the design of market structure is controversial. Ultimately, one's position on the issue is inexorably linked to one's views about the efficacy of competition, one's faith in the ability of the free market to produce socially desirable outcomes, and one's opinion about the efficiency of the regulatory process itself.

Wide-ranging issues regarding the regulatory process are raised in this manuscript. For instance: Given the importance of network externalities in trading, how appropriate is U.S. anti-trust policy for the equity markets? Does the regulatory process facilitate the competitive process, or impede competition because of regulatory capture and the typically difficult, protracted process of getting regulatory approval? How efficient are our markets? How competitive are our markets vis-à-vis newly developed foreign exchanges, most notably in Europe? Has or has not regulatory intervention contributed to the quality of the U.S. markets?

Both regulatory and technological developments have resulted in a mind boggling pace of change for the industry. Since the Zicklin conference, Nasdaq has demutualized. Both Nasdaq and the NYSE have changed from fractions to decimals. Electronic Communications Networks (ECNs) have gained increasing market share and a great deal of attention, not just in the U.S. but also in Europe. Three ECNs have filed with the SEC for exchange registration (Archipelago, Island ECN, and MarketXT) and one of them, Archipelago, has now formed an alliance with the Pacific Stock Exchange. [1] The Nasdaq Stock Market is undertaking the development of an electronic limit order facility (called the Super Montage). Extended hours trading has received more widespread attention. In 2000, the SEC focused its attention on the fees charged by market centers for trade prices and quotations, on market fragmentation, and on the need to display a range of limit orders outside the best bid and offer. In October of that year, the SEC enacted Regulation FD (Fair Disclosure), which requires that all material information released by corporations be made available to all investors at the same time. The efficiency and economic role of a key component of the national market system, the Intermarket Trading System (ITS),[2] is being questioned.

[1] As of April 2001, Archipelago's Exchange Filing was pending SEC approval.

[2] Intermarket Trading System (ITS) is a computer system that interconnects competing exchange markets. ITS is operated by Securities Industry Automation Corporation (SIAC).

While the competitive, technological, and regulatory environment has been changing, the issues addressed, on a fundamental level, have remained the same. As long as there have been exchanges, participants have been concerned about market quality issues such as transparency, fragmentation, liquidity, price volatility, and trading costs. Also of major importance are systemic risk, technological inertia, price manipulation, and other abuses of power and position. But the overriding focus of the conference and of this manuscript is not on the specific issues themselves. Of key concern is the role a government regulator should play with regard to these issues. Should markets, with all their imperfections, be left free to evolve naturally, or should a government agency participate in designing market structure and in writing the rulebook?

The discussions were sometimes heated. In many ways, the debate could have been productively lengthened. Lots of questions were raised, but not all were answered. Hopefully, the reader will appreciate the complexity of the issues, recognise the gravity of the matter, and acknowledge that some of the right questions were asked. Ultimately, the markets and the market participants will tell us whether or not reasonable regulatory decisions are being made today, and whether or not we have the right regulatory framework.

A number of people have been helpful in the preparation of this manuscript, in particular David Arcement, Miriam Humbach and Avner Wolf. In addition, I wish to thank the sponsors who made this conference possible (see page xi).

Robert A. Schwartz

CHAPTER 1: VIEW FROM THE NYSE[3]

William R. Johnston

Rigorous self-regulation is one of the most important reasons behind the success of the U.S. financial markets. Through government legislation, through Securities and Exchange Commission oversight, and through the function of the self-regulatory organizations, the U.S. financial markets have been successful in earning the trust of the investors, and in maximizing participation and liquidity. The success of our own efforts at 11 Wall Street clearly depends on the quality of the regulatory environment created in Washington by the SEC and Congress. Our own role as a self-regulatory organization is a critical part of the NYSE brand name.

With the increasing globalization of markets, the stakes are now higher than ever. We are not just talking about how U.S. investors will trade in the U.S., but also whether the U.S. will retain our leading position in the global financial marketplace. So, here's the challenge. In our dramatically changing financial marketplace, how do we make sure that regulation helps rather than hinders?

Forming an appropriate self-regulatory environment is not a simple task. The major responsibility for change lies with the market centers themselves in concert with the securities industry and government regulators.

In my remarks this morning, I would like to focus on some of the major initiatives currently in process at the NYSE, and tell you what we are thinking about for the future.

When Bob invited me to speak at this conference, he asked if I needed any projection equipment. I requested a crystal ball. Unfortunately, that piece of equipment is not so readily available.

The U.S. financial marketplace is changing in ways no one could have foreseen ten years ago. It is more global. Last year (1998), non-U.S. companies accounted for one of five new listings on the New York Stock Exchange. Ten years ago, they accounted for less than one of ten. Institutional investors are now the biggest players in our marketplace and demand to be heard. Institutions account for about 70% of NYSE average daily trading volume. The marketplace is also more competitive, with new entries like electronic communication networks and alternative trading

[3] Where appropriate, this speech has been updated to reflect events that have taken place since the conference.

systems. At the same time, existing markets in the U.S. and Europe are consolidating via mergers and alliances.

The marketplace is of course more technological, as well. Today, nearly ninety percent of our orders are delivered over our network, accounting for roughly half our share volume. And the other half of the volume – the portion delivered via floor brokers – is done with a level of technological support that many might find quite surprising. In the past few years, we have seen a dramatic increase in online trading by individual investors. According to some estimates, fourteen percent of all trades are now done online. Some of the growth in online trading is clearly related to technology-stock euphoria and the relentless bull market. But aside from these factors, online trading is definitely among the trends of the future. Additionally, we have a more flexible regulatory environment and, under new SEC rules, a greater possibility for innovation and experimentation.

We are entering a period of change in the U.S. financial marketplace that is as significant as any period since the Securities Acts of '33 and '34. It is a time of great possibilities, when old assumptions of what markets should be like are challenged, when your competitor today could be your partner tomorrow, and your challenger tomorrow could be someone who doesn't exist today.

What will be the impact of these changes on the financial markets and our customers? Until that crystal ball arrives, let me offer some insights from the NYSE. I am going to break these down by the three themes of innovation, competition and efficiency. But there is a good deal of overlap among them, because they really all involve asking the same questions; How can we best meet the changing needs of our customers, and where can we bring additional value?

On the theme of innovation, the NYSE is looking at extending its trading hours in connection with our globalization efforts. We entered the decade with fewer than 100 non-U.S. stocks; today we have nearly 400. Non-U.S. stocks account for over ten percent of list, and ten percent of volume. An international list requires more access than the business hours in one time zone can provide. Demand is growing to offer longer hours to trade these stocks, and perhaps the largest U.S. stocks, as well. We are currently exploring with other markets around the world the idea of forming an alliance, in which global stocks would trade around the clock, following the sun. This would grow the global pool of liquidity across the three major time zones: Asia/Pacific, Europe and the Americas.

We want to offer more formats and greater flexibility to the institutional investor, and are looking to trade more non-U.S. stocks in home-market ordinary shares or global shares. American depository receipts (ADRs)[4] will continue to be an important tool for the retail investor. But institutions want seamless trading, the ability to buy Sony in the U.S. in the morning and sell it seamlessly in the evening in Tokyo. ADRs are not fungible; you cannot buy a Sony ADR on the NYSE and sell it in Tokyo. Global shares are designed to make seamless trading possible. You can buy DaimlerChrysler (DCX) in Frankfurt and sell the same security in New York. Going forward, we believe more companies will follow the DCX model; global shares that trade in virtually the same form around the world. In March 1999, we set up a joint discussion with the Tokyo Stock Exchange to see if there is any possibility of a future link between us. The talks are still in the exploratory stage, but thus far we have resolved to have a close exchange of information between markets from now on, and to set up a working committee between us.

The NYSE is also developing new approaches to institutional business. One of them is Institutional Xpress. We are considering offering more direct access to liquidity on the book, and IXP has 3 innovative features to facilitate this. It offers an increased amount of information from floor to institutions, anonymous access to the floor for institutional investors, and under certain circumstances (size and time) it enables institutions to execute directly against the quote.

Already in operation is a tandem of our Broker Booth Support System (BBSS) and our Wireless Data System (WDS). BBSS is a link from the upstairs to the booth and WDS is a mobile extension of that link. Together, they offer a seamless connection from the upstairs trading desk to the crowd on the trading floor. Floor brokers have electronic means to communicate instantly from the crowd, and it provides better, more timely information for the end customer. These new technologies are one of the primary reasons we're moving to a new building in 2004 or 2005. The new building will accommodate growth and enable us to build a state-of-the-art facility.

On the theme of competition, there was news in early 1999 that we were exploring the possibility of trading Nasdaq stocks, which is something we have been thinking about for over a year. This would mean creating an alternative market that combines the best features of an auction market and an electronic system. Every day ten percent of business in NYSE-listed stocks

[4] The American Depository Receipt (ADR) is a mechanism for investment in foreign securities and was first introduced in 1927. Typically with ADRs, an investment bank purchases shares of stock in a foreign company through a foreign exchange and resells certificates that evidence ownership to the foreign security through a US exchange. Transactions, such as issuing and canceling certificates, are usually conducted by depository banks.

prints on Nasdaq; we do none of theirs. We have talked to every ECN[5] and ATS[6] that wanted to discuss the possibility of our entering this business, but have not yet reached any decision. We still could buy, build, partner or do nothing. One possibility would be a hybrid format, both floor and screen based, with multiple dealers upstairs and down, plus a specialist with an affirmative obligation. If we proceed, we're looking to offer something that would consolidate trading in these stocks, not fragment it further.

Going forward, one of the key questions will be that of competition vs. fragmentation. Competition among markets is beneficial in that it spurs innovation and efficiency. But there is risk that in a more deregulated future, the presence of too many tiny niche competitors could fragment the pool of liquidity too far, which could make the process of trading more difficult for institutional investors. As the number of competitors continues to grow, we need to keep a close eye on the quality of the overall market.

The bottom line is the efficiency of markets: how we deliver liquidity quickly and cost-effectively to customers. There are two developments on that front. One is regarding teenies and decimals.[7] Here again, as changes take place, we have to keep an eye on market quality. Since we moved to teenies, we have found that spreads have decreased significantly, the depth at the best bid and offer has decreased, and cumulative depth in the limit-order book at prices away from the inside quote has also declined. The net effect is that liquidity demanders trading orders of less than 10,000 shares are better off, and liquidity demanders trading orders of more than 10,000 shares are worse off.

We are scheduled to go to decimals in the second or third quarter of 2000.[8] The market will determine the increment to use, and that determination may have a substantial impact on liquidity. Whatever the increment is, we will compete. Moving to decimals will multiply the number of transactions,

[5] Electronic Communications Networks (ECNs) are order book systems that electronically match buyers and sellers of stocks without the need for middlemen such as market makers specialists.

[6] Alternative Trading System (ATS).

[7] The Common Cents Stock Pricing Act of 1997 (H.R. 1053) required markets to convert their stock prices from fractions to decimals by June 2000. Implementation was put on hold so any residual Y2K issues could be resolved. All major foreign stock markets use the decimal system.

[8] Decimals began to be phased in at the NYSE on August 28, 2000.

orders, quotes and messages. The system capacity of markets and member firms will have to be ratcheted up accordingly.

Looking at efficiency in another way, we foresee not just greater competition among markets, but greater cooperation, as well. As the industry continues to focus on trading costs, consolidation will increase. For example, the NASD and we share many of the same customers. At some point, we could share some facilities in an effort to save industry money and enhance regulation. However, a larger merger between us is unlikely because of the probable anti-trust implications.

All of these developments will help inform the ongoing discussion of what our markets should look like in the future. Here are a couple of bedrock principles we should keep in mind. Today, U.S. financial markets set the world standard for liquidity, efficiency and integrity. They are not perfect, and they never will be, but they are the best yet invented. Changes in our markets are taking place with all the speed that technology is bringing, and we have to be mindful that changes in markets can bring unintended consequences. When the eighth was broken, there was talk of going beyond teenies to fractions so small no one could decipher them in newspaper tables, much less understand them. We headed that off by announcing the move to decimals. What I am saying is, this must not be a race to the bottom. Everything we do should meet the test of building an ever-stronger marketplace for our customers.

CHAPTER 2: THE BROAD PERSPECTIVE

Moderator – Robert Schwartz
James Angel
Junius Peake
Benn Steil
Hans Stoll
Richard Sylla
Robert Wood
Steven Wunsch

Introductory Statement

SCHWARTZ: This panel will focus on a broad spectrum of issues that pertain to regulation's contribution to the efficiency of the U.S. equity markets.

It has been an era of incredible change. Not just on this side of the Atlantic, but in Europe as well, we see the inter-mixture of competition, technology, and regulation. What has regulation accomplished in this time? Has it helped or has it hindered? Has the order flow consolidated, or have liquidity pools fragmented?

One thing is absolutely clear – the change has been tremendous. I've heard people talk about this change as a revolution. But, in a revolution, it is clear that there is one party fighting another party and you know how things line up. What we are witnessing today is not a revolution. It's an earthquake. The earth is changing beneath us and nobody really knows where we are heading or where we will wind up.

Where are we after all these changes? What about the profits of the intermediaries? Are we comfortable about that, about how the intermediaries stand? What happens if at some time in the future the bull market ends and we get into a flat or bear market? How will the intermediaries feel then? How will we all feel about market structure? What's happening with execution costs? After years of talking about best execution,[9] is there anybody here who can even define the term?

[9] Best execution refers to a broker-dealer's duty to seek the most advantageous terms reasonably available under the circumstances for a customer's transaction. Translating this general concept into an implementable, empirical measure is not an easy task.

What about bid-ask spreads and price discovery? And it's not just the spread itself, but also the depth of the market that matters. What about the initial public offering (IPO) volatility that we've been seeing of late? And what about the level of volatility in general?

The statistics for MarketWatch.com's IPO are given in Table 1. The initial offering price was 17, and the first trade price was 90. Then it went to a daily high of 130. Think about it. If 90 really was the right price and it was issued at 90, maybe it would never have gotten to 130. 130 is as disastrous as 17. Over the full day, there was an 833 basis point difference between the first trade and the closing, and people fight for 30 basis points. But the intraday swings, starting with the $17 IPO price, were enormous. I could get an EKG and put it up there. I think we would agree that the patient is hyperventilating.

Table 1. Marketwatch.com's IPO

Date:	January 16, 1999
Initial price:	$17.00
First trade price:	$90.00
High price for the day:	$130.00
Closing price:	$97.50

Figure 1 presents the picture of a nice, calm, trading pattern for Exxon shares for September 11, 1997. You can see what the spread is as we go from the lower dashed line to the higher dashed line. If you are buying and selling all day long as a specialist, you buy at the lower dashed line, and sell at the higher dashed line. Where it is squeezed down a bit, you go from the dashed line to the dotted line. And that's great. This is the kind of picture we like to see. This is a half an hour in the trading life of Exxon.[10]

[10] Exxon merged with Mobil on November 30, 1999, and is now ExxonMobil Corporation.

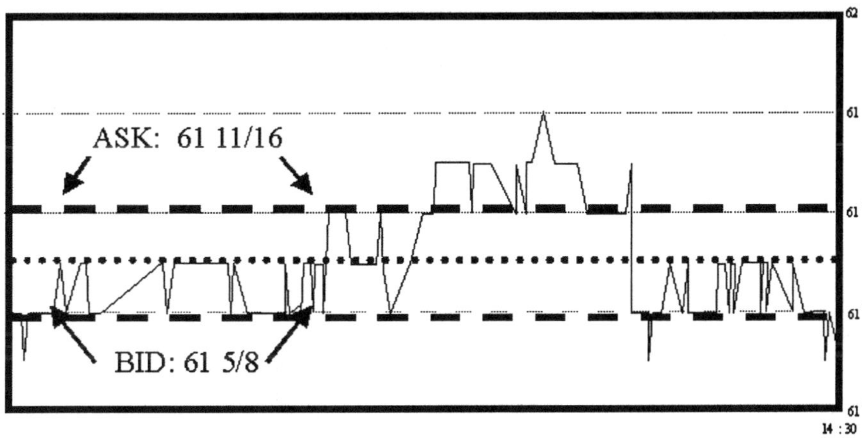

Figure 1. Thirty Minutes of Trading on EXXON, September 11, 1997. Source: Bloomberg L.P.

Now, expand it out to the full day. The picture is shown in Figure 2. The seas get rough. Look at those waves, at those price changes. The box in Figure 2 shows the half-hour period shown in Figure 1. We need a magnifying glass to see the bid-ask spread in the full day picture.

Figure 2. Full Day of Trading on EXXON, September 11, 1997. Source: Bloomberg L.P.

We must get a better feel for what is causing those price swings. Is it news? Is it Exxon specific news? Is it macro news? What's happening with Alan Greenspan and the macro scene? What is going on?

Figure 3 presents a half hour price chart for AOL, and Figure 4 presents AOL's full day price chart. Over a 30-minute period, we can't even see the spread for AOL. Is it in teenies, or eighths? Can you see any bid-ask bounce there at all? The full day for AOL is the worst. Of course, my academic colleagues could say this is casual empiricism at its finest. True. But, you don't have to do much fishing to come up with patterns like this. Many of us have seen trading screens. I don't think they are misleading examples.

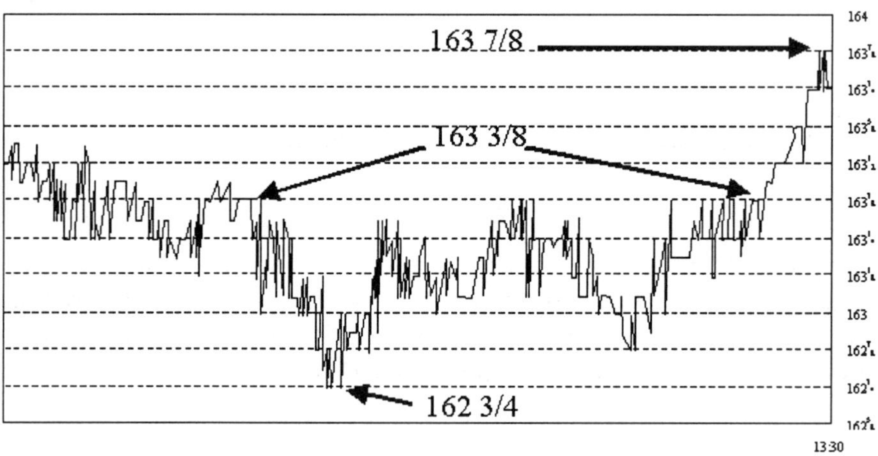

Figure 3. Thirty Minutes of Trading on AOL, February 5, 1999. Source: Bloomberg L.P.

Can volatility be regulated? This question must be addressed. Should we be considering regulatory rules ("thou shalt not be too volatile") or market structure? What causes the volatility? Is it news? Is it information? Is it what we commonly call liquidity trading? Is it institutional investors? The new, on-line retail investors? Momentum players? Or is it an old problem that has been highlighted once again – illiquidity and price discovery in action. Price discovery is a difficult, dynamic, protracted process. One of Don Weeden's traders, Bob Turchyn, mournfully asked me the other day, "How do we discover prices in a crazy, frenetic market"?[11]

[11] Don Weeden is Chairman of Weeden & Company.

Figure 4. Full Day of Trading on AOL, February 5, 1999. Source: Bloomberg L.P.

Panel Discussion

SCHWARTZ: Technology has indeed had a tremendous impact, but how do we fit all the new mousetraps together? Do we look to the regulators for answers, or do we let the markets form naturally? What is regulation's role? That is a key question we are here to address. Bob Wood, could you start off by commenting on volatility?

WOOD: I am interested in the relationship between price discovery and volatility. During the Brady Commission study of the October 1987 crash, October 20th, the day following the crash, was most interesting. We witnessed the largest intraday price increase yet observed on that date, but by the end of the day the market had collapsed back to its starting point. What happened? In my opinion, the market, in the panic situation of the crash, had lost its ability to discover price. Extreme volatility apparently can adversely affect price discovery.

Why are we observing episodes of extreme volatility recently for IPOs and dotcom stocks? Could this be related to weaknesses in the price discovery process? In considering price discovery, we imagine that the market is constantly groping toward the true but unobservable equilibrium price. Is this process inherently more difficult with certain types of stocks? Or do certain types of stocks attract investors that make price discovery more difficult (perhaps momentum traders)?

The dotcom stocks may have a very high option content due to extreme growth opportunities and that could contribute to their volatility because of the complexity of pricing such an instrument. For example, an option grows in value as its volatility increases or, more specifically, the volatility of its underlying asset, which is embedded in the same instrument that is the option. In contrast, equity values decrease with volatility. This valuation complexity may contribute to the volatility of such instruments.

The tools we use to measure volatility are primitive. It would be wonderful if we could develop a metric to measure the interaction of price discovery and volatility that did not assume stationery over an interval where the first moment at least is inherently nonstationary.

SCHWARTZ: On the Brady Commission, one of the main things that you were looking for was manipulation.

WOOD: Yes.

SCHWARTZ: Did you ever come up with a firm opinion about that?

WOOD: We did not find manipulation as such. We did observe incredibly heavy selling from portfolio insurance traders.

SCHWARTZ: Was there any consideration of excess volatility being characteristic of markets, or of accentuated volatility being related to inaccurate price discovery?

WOOD: We looked at volatility over the period from the '20s to where we were at the time of the Commission. We saw periods during the depression where there was huge volatility.

SCHWARTZ: What about today's volatility? In your opinion is it just an old problem that is still with us?

WOOD: I'm not sure. I do know that there have been periods of excess volatility in the past, and I believe we are in a period like that today.

SCHWARTZ: Hans Stoll, you were part of the institutional investor study that focused on these issues.[12] Have the issues changed much, in your opinion?

STOLL: Since working on the institutional investor study in the late '60s, things have changed quite a bit in the market microstructure area. I am not sure if fundamental volatility has changed that much, but the influence of regulators, and what we think about regulatory policy and market structure has changed.

In the 1960's there was one market, the New York Stock Exchange. The competitive issue we were worried about was competition among brokers and dealers within that market. There really wasn't much cross-market competition, although Don Weeden started meddling in the New York Stock

[12] Hans Stoll served on the staff of the Institutional Investor Study of the Securities and Exchange Commission in 1969-70. The Study, which was filed with the SEC in 1971, assessed the competitive structure of the markets, the profitability of specialist operations, and the behavior of major market participants such as the institutions.

Exchange by taking NYSE prices and publicizing them and trading off the exchange.[13]

The watershed event was the 1975 Securities Acts Amendment, May Day, when we de-regulated the Congress and the SEC de-regulated commissions. Before that, the focus had been, "let's put all our eggs in one basket and watch the basket," which was the New York Stock Exchange. Let's assume responsible behaviour and, if something is going wrong, we won't adopt a competitive policy. We will simply watch the exchange more closely.

That changed after '75. The new notion was, we have got to give people access. So the two regulatory principles that I want to contrast are: (1) the principle of competition and transparency, and (2) the principle of free access.

Competition is furthered by transparency, as it was in the '20s. When people were stealing the quotes from the New York Stock Exchange, they were competing because they were able to say they could give the same price as on the New York Stock Exchange.

In the '70s and '80s, the emphasis got transferred to the idea of access and that everyone should have free access. I would like to get us thinking about the contrast between those two principles, and whether they are both equally valid.

SCHWARTZ: Competition could be used to get a better quality of product. But as micro economists, we generally think of competition as a means to drive prices down. What is "the price" in securities trading? It would be commissions. But as soon as you negotiate them, the competition is with regard to spreads. Is that right, Hans?

STOLL: Yes. The issue exists in both areas, commissions and spreads. You want to compete with respect to spreads, and you might want competition among market makers or among markets. I think the way we got to the idea of access and competition among markets is that there was one market maker in New York and you want competition from other market makers in other markets. That competition should go beyond competitive commissions. And so, somehow, we had this feeling that traders and the public should have access to trading in New York Stock Exchange stocks.

But you had NYSE Rule 390 that prohibited New York members from having access to competing markets, and therefore hindering competing

[13] Don Weeden is Chairman of Weeden & Company. In June 1978, Weeden & Company introduced the National Securities Trading System (NSTS), an electronic market managed by a central computer without an exchange floor. NSTS was subsequently bought by the Cincinnati Stock Exchange, and became known as the Cincinnati experiment. NSTS ultimately failed to capture sufficient order flow to remain in operation.

markets.[14] There is a big difference between transparency and competition that has to do with getting information about the quotes in the New York Stock Exchange. Access means the ability to trade in every market. Markets could be fragmented, and still be competing because of information flows. We are at a point now where we are connecting markets. So the two principles are competition and transparency on one hand, and access and market linkage on the other hand.

But, regulatory policy has gone too far in insisting on access and market linkages. You can get a lot of competition simply by transparency. It's not clear that we need to link every market to every other market so that any order can trade in any market. The order can make its decision about which market to go to on the basis of the available information. Without the need to require that if an order goes to one market, it could then be linked to the other market. Have we gone too far in access and linkages? Is it not sufficient to have complete information about the prices in all markets, and let the market decide where to send the order, and let it go to the best market?

SCHWARTZ: Let's get Jay Peake's reaction, and I also want to get Benn Steil's reaction, because Benn has seen some of these similar issues debated in Europe and I think will have a somewhat different response. Jay, what do you think?

PEAKE: I will give you an example of where we are in regulation right now. Supposing that the ATM system ran as follows: You would go to one ATM machine to find out how much money you had in the bank, you would then walk through the rain for two blocks to the next ATM machine to put in the order to get the money out, and you would then walk two more blocks through the rain or snow, to find out what happened, and maybe to get the money. You'd all say the designer of such a system was crazy. But that's what we have in the securities industry today.

You've got a consolidated quote system that tells you what the prices might be, and not all of them are there. You have another system, if it works, called the Intermarket Trading System (ITS) that moves the order around from place to place. Then you have a third system called the Consolidated Tape System (CTS) that tells you what price things traded at, maybe.

That's the result of 25 years of having attorneys in Washington, called the SEC, design systems. What does it mean to have competition between

[14] NYSE Rule 390 prohibited NYSE members and their affiliates from effecting transactions in NYSE-listed securities away from a national securities exchange. On December 10, 1999, the New York Stock Exchange filed with the Securities and Exchange Commission a proposed rule change to rescind NYSE Rule 390. On May 5, 2000 the SEC approved the proposed rule change.

markets? If I were to ask you the price of a stock, would you say it's New York bid, offered at Cincinnati? Of course not. You'd say 25 bid, offered at 25 and 10 cents. We need competition among prices, not among places.

After 25 years, we've got a mess. We've got all sorts of market places out there trying to compete when the buyers want to pay the least and the sellers want to get the most. If you sell a house, do you multiple list it or do you go to a single broker? You multiple list it because you get the most potential buyers for your house. But we have systems where if you put an order in on the Pacific, the odds of it getting executed on the Cincinnati are zero, if they have the best price or not. They may match the price, but it won't be the first bid in at the price.

We have had a Rube Goldberg, Byzantine-type of system for 25 years, and its getting worse every day. We need to clean it up. The NASD is trying. They are fighting a valiant battle. But having pulled everything apart, they are now competing against the systems their own members have built.

In Canada, they have finally come around and said they're going to have a national market system. Two years ago, when I gave a talk in Toronto, I was told, "Jay, great idea, but it will never happen in Canada. Absolutely not. We have different languages, different cultures, we don't have a strong central government. It won't happen." But it did happen, and in less than two years.[15] How about a pan-North American market to compete with the European market that's coming? I think that is essential.

Regulation has got to stop focusing on having lawyers write rules. The SEC has required that prospectuses be in plain English, but obviously they never asked this of the lawyers who issue the releases. I was just reading a release today. I don't understand half of it. And I've been in the business for 50 years. Enough said.

SCHWARTZ: After all these years of technology, of regulation, of conferences, of microstructure research on the part of Hans Stoll and others here, what is the shape of our markets now and why? We can be excited about the job that is being done under difficult circumstances, because pricing and trading stocks are indeed difficult. But where do we stand, and why?

Benn Steil, what does it look like in Europe? Could a panel like this one be held in Europe and what would the insights be?

STEIL: These types of panels are increasingly being held in Europe. I would say that European regulators are certainly not more enlightened,

[15] On March 15, 1999, The Board of Governors of the Toronto Stock Exchange (TSE) announced that the TSE has reached an agreement with the Montreal, Vancouver and Alberta exchanges to restructure the Canadian markets along lines of market specialization. As a result, TSE will become the sole senior equities market in Canada.

generally, than U.S. regulators. But the most important reason why Europe has progressed so tremendously over the past ten years is that there has not been a European regulatory authority to control the cross border competition. What you had was exchanges competing against one another cross border. The competition was not just in terms of market architecture, but in terms of their rulebooks. You effectively had home country control and rule systems competing against each other. Europe has been a phenomenal empirical study backing up Han Stoll's point about information.

You don't have a European SEC. You don't have any ITS. You don't have any CQS.[16] Yet these markets were not fragmented, even when they were competing with one another. Private companies, like Reuters and Bloomberg, play precisely the sort of role that the CQS and ITS would play if they were more efficient. Even when the London Stock Exchange was accounting for about one third of continental share trading, studies have shown that there were no unexploited arbitrage opportunities between Paris and London.

Now, of course, because the exchanges have been forced to compete against one another in order to survive, liquidity has concentrated once again in the home markets. These home markets are now consolidating cross-border because they have all settled on the same basic market architecture – the continuous electronic auction market structure.

Efficiency is currently the route to survival. It's interesting to note that about a third of the European exchanges are now private companies. They are de-mutualized. The shareholder base is becoming much wider than the membership base.

What difference does this make? When you operate an exchange as a mutual association, the members of the exchange are intermediaries for everybody else's transactions. They derive a significant proportion of their trading profits from intermediating others' transactions. Naturally, they have a vested interest in slowing down reforms that reduce demands for their own intermediation services. And so Stockholm, for example, when it became the first exchange in Europe to demutualize, was able to bring in remote, foreign membership, much earlier than the others were. This was because Stockholm's own members could no longer block it.[17]

To give you an idea of how far Stockholm has come, that exchange was on its deathbed in 1991. But now it is a thriving international company and, having been absorbed by OM, the Swedish derivatives exchange operator and

[16] Consolidated Quote System (CQS) collects and disseminates, electronically, current bid and ask quotations along with volume, from and to all market centers trading listed stocks.

[17] In January 1993, the Stockholm Stock Exchange was incorporated as a company, Stockholm's Fondbörs AB, owned in equal parts by the Exchange's members and issuers.

technology company, they have thousands of shareholders. It is itself listed on the Stockholm Stock Exchange. Foreigners own over a quarter of the shares. It has a market cap of about two billion dollars, and could easily be bought out tomorrow by a Reuters, or an IBM. If that isn't a strong incentive for producing efficient markets, I don't know what is.

SCHWARTZ: How has its share price performed?

STEIL: Exceptionally. The share price of the Exchange went up over seven-fold within the first two years of operation. It is a remarkable success story. They knew that their future did not lie with the current members of the exchange, but with investors around the world. They were the first exchange in Europe to allow direct electronic access for institutional investors.

If you ask people at OM what the future of the exchange is, they don't talk just about the Nordic market. They talk about things like trading Motorola, because they believe that they have the best international network in the world for trading telecommunication stocks. They may be wrong, but the important point is that they have the incentive structure right. If they don't pursue the right strategy, they can be taken over by somebody who will do it better. They cannot afford to make mistakes.

SCHWARTZ: The whole issue of demutualization is important and it also becomes involved with the SRO obligations of our market centers; the NASD and the NYSE, for instance. All of the panels will address the issue; primarily Dan Weaver's panel and Maureen O'Hara's panel. We'll definitely want to get back to it.

Now as you were talking, Benn, it led me to think of so many presentations and things that we write, in which we always say there are three things that have driven change in the securities market. There is technology, clearly. There is competition, which comes with new technology. And there is regulation in terms of market structure, which has obviously affected what is going on. The alternative to regulation is to let markets consolidate naturally, and to let transparency be a natural product of systems and of how people behave in the systems. Steve Wunsch, can you talk about markets forming naturally, and about what that implies for regulation?

WUNSCH: We have the strongest markets in the world here in the U.S. and, with all due respect to the Europeans, we will conceivably keep that position. But the secret of our success has not been regulation. While regulation has been useful to prevent fraud and abuse, the secret of our success is that we did not have regulation around when our markets formed. They were able to form naturally.

Now, the problem is that when markets form naturally (and this happens all around the world, not just here), they form in an anti-competitive fashion. Every market forms primarily to enable its members to have advantages over non-members. It's an unlevel playing field from the word go. They fix commissions, they fix spreads, and they fix trading rules that are in their own self-interest. Obviously, this runs counter to the anti-trust body of regulation, which is probably the bedrock regulatory structure here in the U.S.

Hans Stoll talked about May Day being the watershed event. It really was. But that was when we began to usher in anti-trust regulation of stock markets. The result has been, and continues to be, in an accelerating way, negative. This is because anti-trust regulation is doing to the stock markets what it always does – it breaks up networks. Whether it's Standard Oil's pipeline network, or AT&T's telephone network, or the airlines not being allowed to come together and provide a unified service. The results are invariably negative because they don't recognize that the value of the network is in its being a monopoly, if it can be. A telephone is not just a useful gadget with some interesting technology. It is useful because everyone is connected to the telephone. So, if you have multiple competing telephone networks, and your friends and family are half on one network and half on the other network, you have got the wrong friends and family.

We are doing essentially the same thing to the stock market by the application of anti-trust regulations. We are taking markets that were monopolies (the New York Stock Exchange which won by open competition and innovation, Nasdaq which created its own separate form of a niche monopoly, and Instinet which created its separate form) and in the recent reforms, what we've said is that all of them have to break up and allow in multiple competitors, multiple ECNs.

Then we try to cobble together again these new competitors and whatever innovations they might provide, but we are not able to make the liquidity network seamless any more. This is why price discovery disengages from reality. This is the source of the excess volatility that we are seeing in the markets these days.

I might pose a question to my fellow panelists, which is relevant to the issue of volatility. The purpose of the stock markets is to provide secondary market liquidity so that companies can issue stock to investors. There is academic support for the argument that, the more liquid a market is, the more premium you'll pay for the stock.[18] But it seems to me that, for many of the Internet stocks, an illiquidity premium is beginning to develop. Investment

[18] See, for instance, Y. Amihud and H. Mendelson, "Asset Pricing and the bid-Ask Spread," Journal of Financial Economics 17, 1986, pp. 223-249.; Y. Amihud, H. Mendelson and B. Lauterbach, "Market Microstructure and Securities Values: Evidence from the Tel Aviv Stock Exchange," Journal of Financial Economics 45, 1997, pp. 365-390; M. Brennan, A. Subrahmanyam, "Market Microstructure and Asset Pricing: On the Compensation for Illiquidity in Stock Returns," Journal of Financial Economics 41, 1996, pp. 441-464.

bankers and the Internet stocks themselves are trying to withhold shares from the market for the specific purpose of making it illiquid, so that prices can be run up by day traders and the momentum gang, all of whom bought into the national market system concept that brings everyone straight into the market. That just accelerates, not only the IPO volatility, but also volatility generally, and seems to have had an uplifting affect on the market capitalization of these stocks.

If it's true that there is an illiquidity premium strategy coming into the marketplace, what does that say about our underlying beliefs about markets setting prices efficiently? If it is true, could one suggest that regulatory policy be directed toward *removing* liquidity in markets because that will make the stocks go up?

SCHWARTZ: That is an interesting point. We have seen it happen with some stocks. Take MarketWatch.com, for instance. If it hadn't gone from 17 to 90 in one trade, it wouldn't have been included in my comments, and it wouldn't have been written about in the newspapers. It may be a high price to pay in some respects, but you are paying for the sizzle. The sizzle pulls people in.

Let me ask you another question, Steve. We are talking about markets as networks. The concept of network externalities has become a very important term in economics, and it applies to the stock market. I often hear, "why do we need a network for stock trading, because the shares are just passed from one buyer to one seller"? We need a network because price discovery is an important, but tricky and imperfect process. The point is, prices are more efficiently discovered if we have a better network. This is all in the context of what Bob Wood and I were interacting on before about how good is price discovery in today's market? Could you comment on the price discovery function and on how you see it evolving?

WUNSCH: Well, I think price discovery is going backward in terms of its efficiency. Price discovery and liquidity are related items. Sometimes people ask the question, "who is a price discovering client, who is a price taker, and who is going along with the market price? Basically, they're all the same. You need to come up with some means of discovering a good price where everybody, or a lot of people, can get liquidity, otherwise there is a disconnect in the markets.

A call market is the way to consolidate price discovery and liquidity, and there is no major call market out there. But worse than the lack of the call market, is the fact that a hyper-continuous market has developed over the last couple of years because of the new order handling rules. Average trade size has been dropping like a stone, within the last couple of years, to something like a quarter of what it had been. You have Amazon trading twice per second, an average of two or three hundred shares each trade. That is a very intimidating liquidity situation for any institution that trades in institutional size. That is why institutional investors basically avoid that whole market sector. It's the illiquidity premium phenomenon. You can't get into the sector, or you would be afraid to be in it because if you did, you couldn't get out. The disconnect between price discovery and liquidity is becoming severe. The reason why? It's because of the break-up of the network.

The network accomplishes another major function: the matching of savers with companies in need of capital. In other words, it's a capital formation network as well as a liquidity and price discovery network. Under anti-trust principles, we have developed the ultimate atomized market. We've gone from having one specialist or a handful of market makers in each stock, to having thousands or hundreds of thousands of individual investors trading on terminals. The trade size is going down, and the amount of trading is going up. This is causing tremendous instability and extra volatility. This dismantles both the price discovery function and the liquidity function, and ultimately it will dismantle the capital formation function.

SCHWARTZ: If one were to ask, "what do systems such as AZX and OptiMark do"? I would say, "price discovery."[19] It isn't just that your call auctions offer a tighter spread, or cheaper commissions, faster trades, or anonymity. I would emphasize that you provide better price discovery.

Over the years, I have talked to a lot of people about the issue of price discovery, and I have come to the conclusion that the term is not well understood. People use price discovery in the context of, "we've made a trade; we've hit a price; we've agreed." Or "I just sold my house for $250,000 and it's really worth more, but we have a trade. We have discovered a price." There is more that is involved.

I was at Bill Freund's[20] conference at Pace University a couple of years ago and Harold Bradley[21] and I had an exchange about this. Harold said, "I discover price by my orders." I said to him, "What if you enter the market for

[19] The Arizona Stock Exchange (AZX) is an electronic single price auction trading system that is owned by AZX, Inc. The OptiMark electronic trading system (owned by OptiMark Technologies, Inc.) also uses call auction principles. OptiMark currently operates as a facility of the Pacific Stock Exchange and Nasdaq.

[20] Bill Freund, a former Chief Economist at the New York Stock Exchange, is currently Professor of Economics and Director, Center for the Study of Equity Markets at Pace University.

[21] Harold Bradley, formerly Senior Vice President for Strategic Investment at American Century is currently President, American Century Ventures.

Exxon and somebody says, 'Harold, you tell us what Exxon should trade at.'" He jumped back and replied, "Oh, but I can't do *that*." And that's the point I want to make. Price discovery is not any individual's responsibility. It is the market's collective responsibility.

As markets come together to discover price, the system matters and the network matters. But what happens then? We hear the no-no word, "monopoly."

Let me turn to Dick Sylla. As a financial historian and a micro economist, you've been thinking about these issues. What is there about securities markets that makes them monopolies, and how should we approach them if they develop as monopolies naturally?

SYLLA: Jay Peake mentioned that he had been on Wall Street for 50 years. Since I am a financial historian, I have been there for 210 years. Monopoly is one of the oldest issues in security regulation. I just reviewed a book by Stuart Banner called *Anglo-American Securities Regulation: Cultural and Political Roots, 1690 to 1860.*[22] A lot of people didn't know there was a security market before 1860, but it offers an interesting perspective. I haven't heard an issue discussed thus far today, including monopoly, that wasn't discussed in England and America before 1860.

There are some micro economists who say it is information systems that make the markets. And that, after all, is what stock markets are. Security markets are markets in information. They consume huge amounts of information and they create huge amounts of information. Pick up your *Wall Street Journal* any day and look at all the information in it that was created the day before. So, if there is a tendency, as Steve Wunsch referred to it, a natural evolution toward greater monopoly in information markets, there are many good reasons why things should be concentrated.

We have a political problem in this country. All the fragmentation we are talking about is as old as the hills in America. We've always fragmented the financial system. Our banking system is different from any other in the world. There is a real tension here. Maybe an efficient market is a monopoly market and shouldn't be fragmented. But then the politicians jump up saying, "Oh, that's a monopoly, we have to do something about it."

Much financial development was compressed into the years 1790 to 1792, when Wall Street had its first crash. People around this city were very embarrassed, businesses failed, and many went to jail. Today you go to Bankruptcy Court and file Chapter 11, but back then, speculators were dragged off to debtor's prison. So New York State passed a law: no trading of

[22] New York: Cambridge University Press. 1998.

securities was allowed in the streets because everybody gets too involved. No public auctions, no short sales, etc. In response to this law, the brokers met under the famous Buttonwood Tree in lower Manhattan and formed a private club with fixed commissions. The fixed commissions were durable; they lasted from 1792 to 1975. And that was the origin of the New York Stock Exchange.

So, regulation created the movement to form the private club, but the private club (the New York Stock Exchange) had a fixed number of members. In New York, the people who traded on the exchange were also the owners of the exchange. So, they had an interest in building up their seat value. This isn't natural everywhere. In Britain, some people owned the exchange and other people were the traders. The owners invited a lot of people to come in and trade. Britain had about 5,000 traders around the turn of the 20th century, and the New York Stock Exchange had about 1,000. In France, where the government controlled everything, the government only allowed 20 or 30 traders, and sold the seats at very high prices. In London in 1907, the seat price was $2,000; in New York it was $7,500; and in Paris it was $460,000.

This tells you that the structure of the ownership rights of the exchange matters, and that there are monopoly rents in there. The structures we see are not totally natural. The history shows lots of different ones. There may be a natural tendency by reason of order flow and liquidity, for monopolies to emerge, but regulation can help or hinder it, and we all theorize on this. It's important to remember that some of the issues we are discussing are really old issues, and that historical research may bring out some of the answers.

SCHWARTZ: There is a natural tendency for order flow to consolidate and for markets, therefore, to consolidate. You can call it by its modern, positive term, "network externalities." Or you can call it by its older, more negative term, "monopoly." Whichever, when markets come together too closely for the comfort of regulators, they are broken up. But what we then lose are the benefits of the natural consolidation, and it paves the way to further regulation. Regulators say that you must integrate systems, that you must expose orders, that you must do it in the context of a system like ITS. But then it isn't a natural product. A paper by Jeff Davis[23] discussed two innovations that were inspired by or pushed by government regulators. There

[23] Jeffry L. Davis, "The Intermarket Trading System and the Cincinnati Experiment," in Market Making and the Changing Structure of the Securities Industry, Yakov Amihud, Thomas S.Y. Ho, and Robert A. Schwartz, Editors, Lexington Books, 1985.

were some exceptions but, basically, these innovations were not very effective.

Jim Angel, would you talk about how markets form naturally?

ANGEL: In order to understand the structure of the equity market, you have to understand why the equity market has naturally organized itself into clusters of exchanges. Most financial markets have not. The currency markets and the bond markets are naturally OTC markets. Why is this? Why is it that many of the same financial firms that are eager to pay millions of dollars for an exchange seat, trade bonds over the counter? The reason is information. If you go to sell ten million dollars worth of treasury bonds, a bond dealer yawns at the order. If you go to sell ten million dollars worth of stock, most dealers run in the other direction because they think you have information.

Information is the key. No one wants to reveal their trading interest because they know it may move the price against them. But everyone wants to know what everyone else is doing. So traders have naturally formed exchanges for the following reason – the benefits outweigh the costs of putting the market together.

Markets are costly to organize. Not only in terms of bricks and mortar, computer servers, etc., but also in terms of obeying the rulebooks. The rulebook is a very important aspect of the organization of a market. Essentially, organized markets say, "you show me your order, I'll show you mine." The participants believe that they are better off as a result. They believe that this forced disclosure makes them better off because they get the benefits of what other people disclose.

What is a market? It is two things: a rulebook and a trading platform. What we have seen in recent years is an unbundling of those two parts. In the United States, starting with the Exchange Act of '34 going through the '75 Amendments, what we've seen is a creeping nationalization of the rulebook in the United States. Now, it is the attorneys in Washington who set the rules.

We are also seeing a gradual unbundling of the trading platforms. Instead of the traditional floor-based exchange, we are now seeing a multitude of different platforms operating under the same rulebook. Increasingly, it is the regulators who are setting the rulebook. But the trading platforms are allowed to compete because nobody knows exactly what the best trading platform is.

There is no such thing as a one-size-fits-all marketplace. Companies and investors prefer different types of market mechanisms. You can buy milk at a 7-Eleven, you can buy milk in a supermarket, or you can buy milk by the tanker full. These are all very different market mechanisms.

STEIL: The big question you left open was whether any one person or organization knows the best rulebook.

ANGEL: That is a good point. Not only does no one organization know the best rulebook, but the nationalization that has gradually occurred is now facing international competition because of the dramatic collapse of communication costs. This means that the natural geographic barriers that separated countries are much, much lower than they used to be. The SEC can no longer say by fiat, "This is it folks, take it or leave it." Instead, the SEC has to worry about what is going on in Europe, Canada, and elsewhere.

DONALD WEEDEN [From the Floor]: I want to say something to all the students of market structure. Listening to this panel, it all sounds very negative. It seems like everybody is troubled by the volatility of price discovery in the marketplace today. But in my 40 or 50 years on the street, there have been tremendous advancements. The Justice Department came in and said, "We don't like monopolies in our industry. There's no need for them." Congress came in and said, "Competition is the basis of the '75 Act," and they encouraged the use of technology. The combination of these things has allowed our markets to respond to the enormous increase in interest worldwide, and has allowed institutional orders of a size that would have been impossible forty years ago to be executed. They have also allowed the public to come in at $7.00 a transaction and get immediate access to the market. We should be jubilant about what has happened to our markets. We should not nit-pick the little price volatilities that we see. I ask this question to the panel: "Would you like to go back to the way things were? Do you think we would be better off"?

SCHWARTZ: We can look at a glass of milk and see it as being 80% full, or say it is 20% empty. A lot of what we are focusing on is the 20%. But if you think of the problems of making markets, of discovering prices, of handling 300,000 share orders along with retail order flow, it is, as you know, a very difficult job. And the job has become more complex in recent years. So when we are asking, "where do our markets stand now, and where are they heading," what we care about is that remaining 20%.

Time is running out. I am now going to ask each of the panelists for a brief closing statement.

STOLL: I agree with Don Weeden that, since the 1975 Amendments that eliminated fixed commissions, traditional restraint of trade issues have been nicely resolved and we have introduced a lot of competition. But the point that strikes me from listening to my fellow panelists is that we have to cobble together these various markets. As Jay Peake said, there's a mess out there.

But what caused the mess and what is the role of regulatory policy here? The point was made that a *natural* monopoly is great, and let it be natural. But the role of the regulator now should not be to enhance that natural monopoly through linkages. I don't know what the market would look like today if we didn't have the ECN rule,[24] which has generated new markets. That was a regulatory change, and the objective was to connect markets. But the outcome has been confusion.

PEAKE: Should we have air traffic controllers competing at the same airport? Of course not. But can you have competing air traffic controllers at different airports? Yes. The people who really ought to be deciding where their stocks trade are the boards of directors of companies. And exchanges should compete for the right to trade that stock. I've argued for years that listing deals should be for no more than two years (renewable, of course). And if two years later it turns out that OptiMark or Nasdaq or the Pacific or the Cincinnati Exchange is a better place, the board of directors of that company should be able to say that that is where my stocks will trade, because it is in the best interest of my shareholders.

That is the kind of natural monopoly we ought to have. I am not concerned with price volatility, and I disagree with my good friend Steve Wunsch. I would rather have 10,000 people around the world competing to buy and sell the 100 shares, than to have one specialist, in one location, who must be either long, short, or even, deciding what the next price of the stock ought to be.

WUNSCH: Jay Peake and I have been arguing that point for fifteen years or more. I remember saying long ago that even if every man, woman, and child in the universe had a terminal to trade stocks, it would not necessarily produce stable liquidity and good price discovery. I still believe that. We are in the midst of a good test of that now, given that the new regulatory rules are bringing individuals, day traders, and momentum traders into the market. We haven't gotten to include every man, woman and child yet, but we may.

With regard to Don Weeden's comment, I view the glass as 80% empty. I think we are, at a rapid clip, actually emptying out the price discovery, liquidity, and capital formation capabilities of our markets. Of course, it is good fun and good business for a lot of folks who get to free ride off the government's desire to break up the original monopolies. Whether it's the New York auction market or the Nasdaq dealer market, many upstairs firms and many individuals get in there and make a lot of money. But the important question is whether or not the actual functions that our markets need to perform are being served by this forcible break up of what used to be a pretty good functioning set of monopolies.

[24] The ECN Rule is an amendment to the Quote Rule that affects Electronic Communications Networks (ECNs). The ECN Rule, which applies to all orders of 100 shares or more, levels the playing field for individual investors by making prices that were previously hidden from most investors available to the public.

With respect to the need for innovation, I don't think there is any particular innovation with umpteen ECNs all essentially adopting the same structure and facilities. And it is now becoming a regulatory policy to make sure that none of them ever wins again. They must all compete on a level playing field, as if it were some sort of sporting contest.

In the old days, the New York Stock Exchange was a very innovative structure. Then the Nasdaq came along and created another very innovative structure, then Instinet came along and created one, too. Then ultimately AZX and OptiMark and others would have come along and tried to find their niche. But the structure which we are forcing now, multi-party competition, all in the same product, is very counter-productive to price discovery, liquidity, and ultimately capital formation.

SYLLA: In response to the comment from Don Weeden, we should feel good. We do have the greatest markets in the world, and they have really done well for the last 18 years. But, let's suppose that the market falls 20%, or 30%, or 40%. I mentioned what happened in New York in 1792. A 20% drop in the market in about two months time led the State of New York to pass a law that has coloured our financial history ever since. And think of the 1930s. In 1929, people were saying, "our markets are the most wonderful in the world." But what happened in the next three or four years when things didn't work out so well?

Look at this morning's *New York Times* and read about a trader called Tokyo Joe. Tokyo Joe thinks it's wonderful to buy up some stock the day before, and then tout it on the Internet and make a lot of money. People say our markets aren't supposed to work that way, but to hell with that, this is a new era, our markets really are good. Let's not let the optimism of today say that nothing bad could happen around the corner.

ANGEL: Amen to Peake's proposal that the listing companies themselves have something to say about where their stocks trade. Rather than having the SEC go through a torturous examination of a new system, let the companies themselves decide. That would be a great improvement.

There is another point that needs to be resolved – that is, who owns the information? As we have said, this is an information business. The equity markets consume and produce enormous amounts of information, and many people treat disclosure as though it is a naturally good thing. This is not necessarily true. To force traders to reveal their information is like forcing somebody to walk down the street without any clothes. Not everybody thinks that is a good idea.

And to force a marketplace that has invested millions or billions of dollars to give away their price and quotation information at some regulated price, does not fit with the emerging paradigm that gives protection to intellectual property.[25] This is a debate that will have to be addressed in the future. Who owns the information? Who has the rights to it? How much is it worth? How much can they charge for it? These are important questions that need to be addressed.[26]

WOOD: I question that an exchange in the European time zone such as Sweden could compete for equity order flow with U.S. markets. Home base appears to have an information or information processing advantage. Consider what happened with DaimlerChrysler--initially the order flow was concentrated in New York but it has migrated to Frankfurt.

I liked Hans Stoll's distinction between information and access. If the large institutional investors wish to form a club, wherein they trade between themselves and access is denied to the retail investor, we may be better off to allow it, than to force everything through the same spigot. We can be informationally connected without necessarily giving everyone access to every market.

STEIL: With regard to the possibility of Sweden competing with the United States, I wanted to emphasize the following. It is no longer Sweden competing with the United States; it's OM, a public company operating internationally which just happens to be listed on the Stockholm Stock Exchange. I emphasized that over a quarter of its market cap is owned by foreigners. It could be bought out tomorrow in a hostile takeover. It's not Sweden anymore, it's a private company, OM.

With regard to what Jay Peake was saying, I agree with 90% of it, and I think it's extremely interesting. But as a small shareholder of private companies, I want to be able to sell those shares where I want, not where the managers of these companies say I should be able to sell those stocks. So I don't believe that the companies themselves should have any right to dictate where their shares should be traded.

Regarding the power of networks, it is interesting to note that the five largest markets in the world – New York, Nasdaq, London, Frankfurt, and Tokyo – have been the slowest to dismantle the mandatory human intermediation of trades. It is not surprising that in network markets there are enormous first mover advantages. This means two things: (1) that change tends to be slow in coming and (2) that, when it comes, it's absolutely cataclysmic.

[25] Roughly one third of Nasdaq and NYSE revenue comes from selling price and quotes to data vendors.

[26] As mentioned in the Preface to this manuscript, the issue was addressed in December 1999 by the SEC in its release, "Regulation of Market Information Fees" (Release No. 34-42208; File No. S7-28-99).

There have been some seminal events over the past few years. The one I would emphasize involving both Europe and the United States, was DTB's[27] enormous success in competing with floor-based LIFFE.[28] It was based on one event, and I will describe it because it is important to understand. The DTB was stuck on a 35% market share vis-à-vis LIFFE in the ten-year Bund futures contract for about four years, until the CFTC[29] allowed DTB direct access into the United States in the Autumn of 1997. Within two months, traders in Chicago accounted for 20% of total ten-year Bund future trading in Frankfurt, and LIFFE Bund futures trading collapsed within three months after that. DTB went up to a 99% market share because they were able to expand their network, whereas LIFFE was not. It's the power of an expanding network.

Internationalization of the markets is very important. It is now necessary to consider what is going on abroad. – Even though the SEC doesn't allow direct access for foreign exchanges, European exchanges already have indirect electronic access via their own members' screens. – With regard to international accounting standards, the SEC no longer has any say whatsoever in the accounting standards that companies use to access U.S. capital. A company can list on a non-U.S. exchange and then have virtual direct electronic access to U.S. investors in the United States. Their home regulatory authorities determine their accounting standards, not the SEC.

SCHWARTZ: Our time is up. It has been a most informative session. Thanks, panelists.

[27] In 1998, two electronic derivatives exchanges, Deutsche Terminborse (DTB) and the Swiss Options and Financial Futures Exchange (SOFFEX) agreed to merge into Eurex, a fully electronic derivatives exchange using common rules and regulations and a joint clearing house.

[28] London International Financial Futures and Options Exchange (LIFFE).

[29] The Commodity Futures Trading Commission (CFTC) was created by Congress in 1974 as an independent agency that regulates financial and commodity futures in the United States.

CHAPTER 3: VIEW FROM THE AMEX

Richard F. Syron

This is an interesting time in many ways, and it has been a busy last few days in my life. So you'll have to excuse me if what you get is a little bit of stream of consciousness and retrospective, with hopefully some view of the future.

Actually, one of the reasons I'm leaving the American Stock Exchange® in New York and going back to Boston is that I was quite horrified—when I was there recently—that people told me I was losing my accent. I suspect there'd be very few people in New York that would have that view, but it does say something about the parochialism of Boston, despite its presence in the financial structure of this country.

The five years that I've been at the Amex have been an interesting busy changing time in a lot of ways. Some evidence of how much times have changed is that not long ago, I was trying to hire Bob Schwartz to conduct some research showing how much better trading would be on the Amex than on the dealer market. So, he, in maybe a minor way, could be a loser on transaction costs itself as a result of our merger with the National Association of Securities Dealers, Inc. (NASD®).

It comes down to the issue of transaction costs. Being an economist myself, I always like to think of things working in this "non-frictionalist" world, but whether there are transactions or not, whether there are transactions *costs* or not, there are lots of frictions in the world. I guess that's the difference between an engineer and a physicist, knowing that things don't exist in a vacuum with no friction. I think some of that can be applied to the securities industry, which I've gotten to know reasonably well in the last five years. I've made a lot of friends in this business. And now, I will be a direct customer, in a different way. My comments here are from the perspective of my current seat at the Amex, not my future role at Thermo Electron.

This has been, as I said, a period of enormous change. Another indication of that—and a lot of things that have happened since then—is that if we look back maybe 18 months to the time when Frank Zarb and I first started talking about "Nasdaq-Amex," it was a little bit like asking, "How would you merge Northern and Southern Ireland?" which is appropriate for this day. It just seemed to be such an "out-of-the-box" approach to things, that I like to think it kicked off some of the change that has started to happen. But it pales in comparison to so many of the things that are going on now.

I can't help but think of some of this from a "big picture" perspective, if you will, and from the perspective of regulation, which is extraordinarily important. Regulation becomes a more and more important obligation of financial markets in the United States for reasons I'll get to, whether those markets are exchanges, market places, or whatever you want to call them. But we face real challenges in that regard because of the interesting juxtaposition of what I would call "societal trends" and "technological capabilities."

Now, from the biggest picture perspective, you would have to say that the dominant trend, or development, in the U.S. economy in the last quarter century has been the shift in power away from the producer to the consumer. This is a terrific economy in which to be a consumer, as everyone notes when they look at what's happening to real disposable income, and then look at what's happening to inflation. But when you talk to anyone who is running a business, including the one I'm going to, they talk about pressure on margins and things like that, which are making it a lot tougher to be a producer. That means it's become a lot tougher to be a producer if you are a stock market, too, whether you're a listed market or a dealer market, and that has some real implications going forward.

The other major factor in all this, are the extraordinary developments we've had in the silicon chip and in what the chip has done. For instance, I was just looking at the latest, three-pound computer—they're almost toys now. They have so much more power than the first ones that were housed in very, very large buildings. This has raised some interesting implications for markets, and for the regulation of the markets. Now, because of a number of the changes that we're seeing societally, and the shift in power away from the producer to the consumer, we've had to do a great deal of restructuring in our economy. The U.S. has been, almost singly at this point, among the major industrial powers successful at this. Part of that restructuring has been to remove some of the traditional intermediaries between the household sector and the investment sector.

The clearest example of that is the relative decline of the defined benefit pension plan and the greater importance that everyone has put on 401Ks and investing for themselves. You know, for better or worse, everyone has to become an investor now. We've all seen the reports about equities being a greater part of the household balance sheet than real estate for the first time since we've had the data. There has been an extraordinary increase of penetration into people's everyday lives. That makes it all the more important that markets be carefully regulated. I think it's hard to disagree with that, and in a time when more and more people are directly exposed to what happens in the markets, attention to it will increase, not diminish.

A quarter century or more ago, the stock market's performance both in its fairness and actual overall performance, made the difference in someone's retirement as to whether they drove a Chevy or a Buick. Now, it's going to make a difference in whether they're able to retire at all. Or, whether they will be able to retire at 65, 68, 72. Or, if you were recently at Goldman-Sachs, at 32. This really does make the fairness and efficiency of these markets much more of a public and political issue than it has been, historically, in the United States. That's the broad societal thing that comes from macroeconomics.

Sometimes we get a little too caught up on discussions of institutional versus retail markets. Individual investors—and it may be concentrated in some cases to a small number of individual investors—still own about 50 percent of equities in the United States, and people are directly exposed to the performance of individual companies on the margin. On the margin, it makes it easier to explain why you've got to make change in order to make the economy more efficient. And so, for that reason and many others, the retail investor is still quite important. We would be making a mistake, for broad societal reasons as well as and, ultimately, for financial reasons, to not have the SEC say that we are the advocate of those that are least able to advocate for themselves. Given technological developments, we clearly have a situation, now, where we can "unbundle" many of the tasks that used to be done at one place and time. I mean, lots of us work all the time now, anyway; that's one of the great advances of technology, isn't it? You can work at home on Sunday afternoons and then, when you go to the hockey game, they can get you on your cell phone. Technology's wonderful. We've been able to unbundle things and re-assemble the pieces that used to have to exist under one roof.

Obviously, that has very, very strong implications for the traditional securities markets. I would go so far to say—and I suppose it's easy to say this when you're about to switch jobs—that the old model doesn't work. The existing model of either an exchange or a market place doesn't work. I like to think that it was some recognition of that, by both Frank Zarb and myself, that led us to believe that we needed to merge the Amex auction market with the Nasdaq dealer market into one company to see what things were going to look like in the future. You simply cannot overemphasize the need to look at this in a "thinking outside-of-the-box" sort of way.

We all like to go around saying we love change. Forget it. We only love change when impacts someone else, but benefits us. I'll tell you my ten-year-old doesn't like the idea of change in terms of moving. We don't like change when it affects us.

We're all creatures of habit when it comes to things like this, and this is going to be an enormous challenge all through this industry, starting with the traditional exchanges and market places. But I would say that there is evidence of hope here, of people being willing to take and make change.

When we first announced this merger of the NASD and Amex, there were a lot of pretty heated calls to my office, to my house, and to any place else that people could get me. The calls were from people who had been used to doing things in a traditional way. The questions included, "What are you, out of your mind?" and "What does this mean?" But, it's very interesting that when we started out, we had probably 35 to 40 percent support to get the vote that we needed to do the transaction. In the end, we wound up with 76.4 percent for and 23.6 percent against. That is, more than three out of four people on the exchange supported doing it.

The big challenge for this industry is how soon can it make the change before we reach the edge of the abyss. You can say it would be a lot better if we did this a quarter of a mile or half-mile from the abyss. But, if we wait for the abyss to yawn, we're going to be in big trouble because, despite some lack of efficiency in U.S. capital markets and despite the problems that have occurred overseas, there are a lot of people over there that are looking at what's developing here. They are looking at the possibility of penetrating our markets, too. We will not necessarily be world dominant in this industry forever. We found that out with autos. We're not immune to that factor.

Now, let me tell you why I believe the traditional model for exchanges doesn't work. The traditional model, as we all know, is to have membership organizations competing with other membership organizations. Now, we could afford to be in that kind of cumbersome situation when we only competed with each other; when like competed with like.

But then along came a lot of other people who realized there were other ways to do some of this. And you know what? They realized that three or four of us could sit in a room at the end of a day when things are developing, and decide how we were going to change and what we were going to do with things. They realized that we could make the change and start to do it next week, without having to go first to the committee on this, and then to the subcommittee on that. We wouldn't have to get membership votes or do any of those things.

Organizational structure has put traditional markets at a real disadvantage in responding to change, and this is something that is going to have to be looked at. Governance is one of the chief issues that the traditional markets have to face. There is another issue that, in its own unique way, fits in to this, and it characterizes traditional markets. It is the enormous degree to which we engage in cross subsidies and imprecise pricing of a product. I was quite shocked—and I didn't think the Amex was much different from anyplace else when I came there five years ago—when someone came up to me and said, "We need to build three more posts."

I said, "OK, what's that going to cost?"

They said, "It's going to cost $22 million dollars."

"What's the return on the investment in the post? Hello?"

"The return on the investment in the post is that the guys say they need it."

I said, "Well, what do we make on these posts or what do we make per post per year?"

"We don't have that data."

We don't have that data because we don't have cost accounting systems that generate any of those things, because we've always been this kind of a service organization. Now, I'm sure that our new competitors can tell us when they look at a piece of equipment what the return on investment of that equipment is at any time. I know that the company I'm going to looks at the different product lines it's in and has all kinds of data on return on investment and hurdle rates and everything like that.

That's one reason the traditional model doesn't work. To some extent, we've been heavily engaged in cross-subsidizing, and not only within product classes of one type of equity as compared with another type of equity. We might be talking about how much they trade or the liquidity of the individual instruments. But what about, within exchanges, across product classes, from equities to options in some cases, or from options to equities in other cases. Perhaps most dramatically, and where it is relevant to this issue, is a very substantial cross-subsidy from the trading side of what we've done, to the regulatory side of what we've done.

Let's face it. When you strip everything away, all that we've done is that we've had a hidden tax. We effectively have charged more for transactions so that we could provide what has been an extraordinarily important service as an SRO; that is, we also regulate the market place. The only problem with that is now we compete with new entities that don't have to conduct that service, that regulation, or don't have to do it to the same degree.

So, that model doesn't work. It's like most hidden taxes. Ultimately they don't work. Something happens in the micro-structure that bubbles up and turns around and makes you have to face the reality that you've got to do this much more directly. We now operate in a world in which you turn on any of the financial news shows as you get up in the morning, and you read the papers, and you look at the screen, and everyone's saying, "We'll pay you $4.92 per trade to trade your stock." That model just doesn't work when you've got to take from what the traditional exchange charges and pull a piece of that off to pay for all the things the SEC wants us to do. We're going to have to find a way to pay for those things explicitly. Now, having said that, I happen to believe that paying for those things is extraordinarily important, because no one complains about the fairness and efficiency in a broad sense as long as the market is on this kind of a rocket ship that's going up like it has been. We just wait and we listen—never mind the financial chat screens—we listen to the radio talk shows.

But, if we get a correction in this market, people will start to say, well, this is the kind of *advice* I got, and this is the sort of *execution* I got. This was the story on this mutual fund, and this is what I thought I was buying, but this is what I may have ended up buying. If there is a correction in the market, then "we ain't seen nothing yet" compared to the questions that are going to be raised in *that* kind of environment.

I'd like to raise a particularly thorny question. I won't provide an answer to it, because it ultimately is one of those philosophical questions that comes back to the question of freedom in society and how you decide to balance safeguards with how much freedom you can have.

Earlier this winter, I was with my wife and kids, and a whole bunch of families from the town I live in. We went skiing in Italy, right on the French border, about the time of the avalanches there. My wife was thoroughly horrified when we talked to the guide that was going to work with this bunch of 14-year-old kids that were with us. There was all that new testosterone that 14-year-old boys have, and how aggressively they want to ski. My wife asked the guide where he was going to let these boys ski with all the avalanches going on. He said to her, gruffly, "You must understand. You must be free to die if you go on the mountain. We cannot regulate this. You must be free to die. That is part of the experience." My wife turned a lighter shade of white than the snow as we went forward. But part of investing is that you must be free to lose, not only free to gain.

The final point I want to make is the interesting challenge that is in front of all of us with day trading. I'm not opposed to this, but with the extraordinary ease that day trading implies, we must ask, when does day trading cross the line and become so addictive that we need a "day traders anonymous" group?

I find it a little scary when I talk to people who say, "I used to be a plumber, or I used to do something else, and I lost my job, but you know, I found this thing and I got this service."

"And what do you do now?"

"I trade."

Just think of this in terms of Americans' normal addiction for doing things that give them an instantaneous response. I must confess to a little bit of this myself. When I made the announcement of the career change I was making, I couldn't help but look at the screen continually to see what happened to the stock of the company I was going to. But we're all that way. So, you take our need to know, immediately, what's going to happen and you combine that with the technological and financial ease of doing it—because of the wonderful accomplishments in giving all people access to the market— and you wonder where you go.

Suppose we're in a situation where you're able to sit in your living room on a Sunday, and you've got your PC on the coffee table and a football game on the TV screen. And, you are able to interact with a giant pool someplace to say, " It's third and eight, we're down by 14 points, there's six minutes left in the third quarter. Is he going to throw long or are they going to throw a post at him?" Suppose you're able to type it in right there and know an instant later what the results are going to be. Now, you can double up your bet. You can decide what *you're* going to do.

That might be something that a lot of people would find addictive. I'm not saying that in the sense of freedom in our society we should constrain people's ability to do things. But we do face an interesting challenge that technology has enabled; we are forced to address questions of regulation and questions about suitability and how we want the markets to work, much earlier than any of us ever anticipated. That is the big challenge facing all of us.

CHAPTER 4: IMPACT ON THE TRADING DESKS

Moderator – Erik Sirri
Mike Cormack
Paul Davis
E.E. (Buzzy) Geduld
William Harts
Mike Murphy
Aldo Parcesepe

Introductory Statement

SIRRI: Before I begin, I must issue a disclaimer. Anything I say today represents my own point of view, not the opinion of any of my colleagues at the Securities and Exchange Commission or any of the Commissioners.

I will start by highlighting a few of the biggest regulatory changes that have taken place in the equity markets over the past few years, and say what I think are the pertinent issues surrounding these changes. There are two that I will be speaking of today; obviously there are a lot more than that.

First are the order handling rules, which went into effect a few years ago.[30] There are two components to these rules. The first is called the "limit order display rule." That rule says that if the market maker is holding a customer order, then he must display that priced order in his quote. That represents a change from how some of the markets used to work. Customers can opt out if they want to, but the requirement says market makers have got to let customer orders show through.

The second is something called a "quote rule." The quote rule says that if a market maker places a better priced quote in an ECN, then one of two things must happen. If that ECN is what we'll call a compliant ECN, then the market

[30] As a result of two academic studies (Christie and Schultz (1994) and Christie, Harris and Schulz (1994)), on January 20, 1997, the National Association of Securities Dealers Automated Quotation (Nasdaq) system began a phased implementation of new Securities and Exchange Commission (SEC) order-handling rules designed to increase the access of individuals to the Nasdaq market and to reduce individuals' transactions costs. The order-handling rules were implemented for the fifty most active stocks on January 20, 1997, for the next fifty most active stocks on February 10, 1997, and for the next fifty most active stocks on February 24, 1997.

maker is okay. What I mean by compliant is that the top-of-book of the ECN shows through into the quote montage. Then the market maker is fine.

If the top-of-book of that ECN does not show through into the quote montage, then the market maker must update his or her own quote. What is the point of a rule like that? It is to prevent the creation of what might be called an inside market. If market makers are willing to buy or to sell at better prices than in the public market, the SEC's view was that the public prices should reflect those better priced quotes.

More recently, we passed a rule called Regulation ATS.[31] In my view, that rule solved a problem of regulatory arbitrage. In effect, some of the SEC's rules were being arbitraged by new entrants. These entities, whether you call them ECNs or something else, were performing functions that most people would consider very similar to the economic functions of an exchange. However, they weren't regulated as exchanges. Regulation ATS was an attempt to rationalize that landscape. Reg ATS accomplished three or four things, which I will run through very briefly.

First, Reg. ATS clarified that if you were a broker/dealer who operated a crossing network or an internal broker/dealer auto-execution system, even though you were deemed to be an exchange, you would be exempt from a lot of the rules that came under Reg. ATS.

Second, Reg. ATS said that if you operated a system that did 5% or more of the volume in a particular stock, the top-of-book of that system must be visible to, and accessible by, the public. It said that you had to comply with the priority rules and all the other rules of the Exchange to which you linked, and it clarified that you didn't really have very many surveillance obligations.

Third, Reg. ATS said that if you do 20% of volume or more, then you have a higher level of responsibility. You have to provide fair access to your quotes. That is, you can't discriminate unfairly as to who can have access to your prices. You can set rules, for example, that restrict on credit quality, but you can't say, "I don't like the way you do business so I'm not going to give you access to your quotes, but I will let you have access to my quotes."

Fourth, Reg. ATS said that, as an ECN, you could choose to register as an exchange. And some of these entities have been talking in the paper about registering as exchanges.[32] There are a couple of benefits to that. You get

[31] Regulation ATS (Alternative Trading System) was created by the SEC as an incentive to allow new markets to start without excessive burdens. An ATS must file with the SEC, regularly maintain records of transactions, and refrain from using "exchange," "stock market," or similar terms in its name.

[32] Island and Archipelago did subsequently apply to register.

tape revenue, and you get to set some of your own regulations as an SRO. And since you haven't existed before, you have the option of demutualizing or being for profit.[33]

Overall, the Commission has emphasized the potential for increased competition between market centers, and has made it easier for new entrants to come in and provide execution services.

The last panel threw down the gauntlet as to whether we have been doing the right things. They disparaged some of my legal colleagues down in Washington, D.C., and that's fine. But, Bob Schwartz is an artful guy. He was very careful to make the regulator the moderator, thereby muzzling the regulator.

Panel Discussion

SIRRI: I'll start with Mike Cormack on the buy-side. Let me ask you a straight forward question. If you believe that the SEC has been favoring the entry of new kinds of competition and has been levelling the playing field, then what has been the effect on your ability to get trades done? Has the resultant multiplicity of trading venues helped you or hurt you on the desk?

CORMACK: It has helped us unequivocally. There was a lot of criticism in the first panel about what the SEC has done. From our perspective, the benefits of their involvement go straight to the bottom line of our shareholders, and we are very pleased. The access provided by the order handling rules has lowered the bar and lowered our rates. The market data we get, as far as market impact cost, always a debatable point, indicate that new alternative trading systems are performing as well as or better than more traditional alternative trading systems that were charging us higher rates. Net, our shareholders are much better off.

In reference to fragmentation, we received over 600,000 F.I.X.[34] indications of interest[35] from our broker/dealers during the first eight months of 1998. Eight years ago, those same broker/dealers were trying to reach us telephonically. Maybe not with this gross amount of indications, but it was

[33] This provision also opened the door for the major market centers, the NYSE and Nasdaq, to demutualize.

[34] Financial Information Exchange.

[35] An indication of interest is a bid/offer sent by a broker dealer to its institutional clients electronically.

still a lot. And it was impossible to effectively manage this information. With 400 market makers in existence, how many firms, or how many broker/dealers, should a money manager like American Century have to do business with, to make sure that we get all of the liquidity we need for our shareholders? Five hundred? A thousand? And what about a retail investor? How many firms do they have access to? The point is there is a lot of information coming in and before the order handling rules of 1997, it was very difficult to access it.

In addition, the order handling rules of 1997 flattened out the playing field among alternative trading systems dramatically. We changed our business mix accordingly, and now we do anywhere from 20% to 35% of our trading using alternative systems or non-traditional systems. This resulted in a 21% reduction in explicit commission costs for our shareholders for 1998, because we used "cheaper" alternative trading systems, and a net savings to American Century's shareholders of two million dollars. That is independent of any sort of market impact cost.

But, once again, those are real savings for our shareholders. Would we have been using the same old alternative trading systems in 1998 that existed in 1997, if those opportunities had not been present? Yes. And we would probably have paid a higher rate for it. So competition is good.

SIRRI: Any drawbacks in terms of the complexity? How difficult is it to get your work done? Does having more systems make it harder to get things done?

CORMACK: There has been added complexity. There are a lot of institutions that are against the new SEC rule that requires institutions to display the orders that they post on alternative trading systems. We have been supportive of that, but some of the SEC rules have changed the business mix. You can see how many alternative trading systems there are now. How many screens should any of us have to look at to find out what the right price is? Fifteen?

There are already at least ten ECNs out there. Do I have to have ten relationships with ten ECNs on the desk top, and then point and click through each one of them? We get literally hundreds of orders a day. The effect of that is mind-boggling. Logistically it's impossible. So, from a logistical standpoint, the move toward a quasi central limit order book (being able to see where the best bid and offer are at any one time), and the fact that the SEC requires people to post these quotes, has benefited us.

The order display requirements have effectively solved this problem though. By requiring disclosure of all orders in the public quote display we can see where the liquidity is and route to those various liquidity pools using alternative trading systems.

SIRRI: Let me jump gears a little. Buzzy Geduld, you operate a different kind of trading desk. Have the rules made your job tougher? Have they improved the market from your perspective?

GEDULD: There has been a tremendous amount of change for a firm like Herzog, and for the whole industry. For one thing, there's the labor costs involved. We found that a market maker could no longer trade as many stocks as he used to be able to trade. It's a lot more labor intensive, which is kind of incredible in this world of computerization. Secondly, the SEC has now asked us to buy at ten, sell at ten, prohibit a profit, and be guaranteed a loss because it costs you money to clear that trade.

SIRRI: You mean to say you guys are losing money?

GEDULD: On those trades, absolutely. We haven't spoken about volatility and how that's affected the institutions. After all, the institutions are the public, not the trading desk. The new order handling rules have given us tremendous transparency and the public certainly benefits from that. But one has to pose the question, "is the public better off with much smaller reports and much more volatility"?

Just to give you an example, we do several kinds of business at Herzog. One is institutional, and one is electronic brokerage – that is, the E-Trades, the Ameritrades, and the A.G. Edwards of this world who are connected to us via computer and who receive instant trade execution. Prior to the order handling rules, we would guarantee a broker an execution of anywhere from 1,000 to 5,000 shares on the inside market.[36] After the order handling rules, we guarantee anywhere from zero to 1,000 shares. So, of course, the question is, is the greater transparency worth it? It may very well be. But there have been major changes. The institutions I speak to are frustrated by the costs resulting from the increased volatility.

MURPHY: Can I say something? It is interesting that you talk about labor cost because I think we're going through this period where we are all going to add lots of computers to make our jobs more efficient, and then were are going to have to add lots of people to work the computers until we all become comfortable with that process.

But Buzzy Geduld and Mike Cormack are right. The volatility has increased. I think the traditional working order given out to a broker is going to become a thing of the past if the markets continue this way. This is because of the volatility, and because of the hundred share markets. More and more, we are looking for a natural buyer and a natural seller, if possible.

[36] The inside market is the national best bid and offer on the market.

Like a lot of others, we're being forced into using the ATS systems. There are a lot of different types of business done. It's a problem that Nasdaq has had to deal with for years. It's hard to find one particular system that does it all. But as we become more and more comfortable with technology, it's going to be a way of life. I mean, you can shoot the innovators.

HARTS: I have no doubt that American Century has lowered it's commission cost by using different ATSs, but a lot of research has shown that commission costs and fees are actually a small percentage of the total cost of doing a trade.

PARCESEPE: I am interested in the functionality of the marketplace. I want to look at some of the things that we have implemented in the marketplace so far. I am in favor of transparency rules, but I don't think they should be mandated. I'd like to give the customer a choice. Next, there are order handling rules and the way they are implemented. The SEC said, "Okay, display the orders." But no one ever took the time, including Nasdaq, to say, "How do we display them?" So what do we do? We display them on the same system with the ECNs.

It reminds me of the most democratic form of government, which is in Italy. When you go to vote you get a choice of 40 parties, but in the last 50 years they've had 60 governments. When you look at the Nasdaq screen, and see 40, 50 or 60 market makers and are not able to get to them, it causes a mad rush for the door. And you cannot accomplish your objectives.

SIRRI: But don't you think that is a short run problem?

PARCESEPE: Let me continue. No one is solving it. So the fact is we're in a defensive mechanism, Buzzy and I and everybody else, because of the mandatory obligation it's just your own order quote. You are on cruise control.

MURPHY: But we have that same problem. It's not just the sell-side. Our positions are as big or bigger than yours.

PARCESEPE: They're much bigger than mine.

MURPHY: So we are all in the same boat.

PARCESEPE: I understand that, but that is why I'm saying it's about the functionality. I think we should address the functionality. If you look at the SEC order handling rules, they are fine. I am in favor of transparency. But if you look closer, you see that you're asking for a market maker to act as a principal market maker on one side, while at the same time acting as an agency representative on the other side. I don't think that's good for the marketplace.

SIRRI: Actually, whether you do that or not is your business. I mean you choose to be in a business where you fill those two roles.

PARCESEPE: What other choice do I have? I have to either display an order in my quote or give it to an ECN. The ECN, by the way, only acts as agent. The ECN is being allowed the courtesy and the right to display its quotes along side the market makers. But the ECN is a part-time participant because if it is not there, there is no market.

CORMACK: Why would you not want to display it?

PARCESEPE: I do, Michael, I do. I just want a method to it. We don't have a method. You are asking me to compromise my daily workings by saying, I am in a proprietary mode, ten to a quarter, proprietary on both sides. Then you say, okay, you've got a 500 share order – and I want to display the 500 shares – you offer 500 shares at ten and one eighth and now you are in an agency mode. So now, when you call me, I have to be in a proprietary mode unless you specifically say otherwise. I'm saying the ECNs are in an agency mode continuously. So they don't have this quandary of going back and forth, capital commitment versus order handling. Nasdaq has not provided the trading community with a system whereby we can either segregate the two or distinguish between the two. If you look at a Nasdaq screen today, it's nothing but mass confusion.

SIRRI: Who is it you think should provide the functionality that you want more of? Is it the SEC? Is it Nasdaq? Is it the private people who've yet to enter?

PARCESEPE: We have a Nasdaq system that has the capacity to be on the Internet and to be driven by its participants, but it's not. They are giving us the same functionality that they instituted in 1970, which is to display a quote on the screen. What other functionality does Nasdaq have? It doesn't provide first come-first serve, central location, or electronic interface. But the private ECNs do.

GEDULD: Structural change and the economics have not caught up with it yet, but I think fees are coming. And I hope they are coming and I think they will.

SIRRI: Could you explain what you mean when you say fees are coming?

GEDULD: There is a proposal before the SEC to allow a second acronym, and that would address the problem Aldo Parcesepe is talking about. I'd be able to display my proprietary market, 19 to an eighth, and I'd lay that market to an institution, to anybody else, and I'd put my own capital up. I'd have a second acronym, and in that acronym, I would be able to display only agency orders. So, if I had 400 for sale at 19 and a teenie, I'd show 400 at 19 and a teenie.[37] Hopefully, part of that second acronym would be my ability to charge a fee just as any ECN does. That would level the playing field and

[37] A teenie is1/16th of a point.

allow firms that have dropped stocks because of lack of profitability, etc., to get some income back. Then we would commit more capital and would have a little less volatility. Having a second acronym would solve a multitude of problems.

SIRRI: Paul Davis, what have you seen happening?

DAVIS: Let me address the issues not only from the trading desk but also from the portfolio management side. The impact of the new order handling rules and the growth of the ECNs has been mixed for us. It has been very positive for the portfolio strategies that require many small bets, which is a large, quantitative part of our business. Those small bets are now easier to put in place. ECNs can be used in conjunction with the Super Dot and, zap zap, at very low cost, all the positions are there.

On the other side of the coin, we now have a situation where day traders are looking for trends and price discovery is happening in a way that is in some sense different from the way that we are trying to discover price. And we are looking for mis-pricing from a volume point of view. The question is, if we get these portfolios in place, how well do they perform? Performance is not as good as it was in the past. So, there is a question for us about the effectiveness of putting these big portfolio positions in place. It goes to price discovery, which the first panel talked about.

What does price discovery mean? What is a good price? Going back to efficient market theory in the '60s, there were some very simple tests to measure how good price discovery was. It's time to revisit them, and reproduce some of those studies, and see what they tell us. It would be interesting.

What can be done from a regulatory point of view? It's great now that we have all these electronic locals that are driving price along with the major institutions. Maybe it's time for the SEC to seriously promote an alternative market structure. Perhaps a call market for Nasdaq stocks.[38] It would make a big difference. I am thrilled that they've supported the evolution of an order-driven market within a dealer market.

Look at when London was trading French stocks and London was mostly a dealer market. The French came out with an order-driven market, and most of the liquidity went back to France. So market structure is important here. But what type of market is better? I always thought a dealer market was more for

[38] A call market, or call auction, enables trades among multiple parties by determining the amount of buying and selling interest for a stock at each possible price and at a pre-specified time, executing all crossing orders at a single price, the value that maximizes the number of shares that trade. For further discussion, see *Building a Better Stock Market: The Call Auction Alternative,* Robert A. Schwartz editor, Kluwer Academic Publishers, forthcoming.

trading start-up stocks, when you couldn't find the liquidity in another way. Should Intel be traded in a dealer market? I'm not sure.

The order-driven markets in Europe are all coupled with call markets. They go hand in hand. I asked somebody, how do you open stocks in Europe? He used the phrase "book building." "What is book building," I asked? My friend replied, "Well, we try to find the price that clears the maximum number of shares." That sure sounds like a call market to me.

The SEC has been focused on the retail investor, on the continuous market, and on levelling the playing field. Unfortunately, this focus has been at the cost of price discovery. There is a way to re-focus. It shouldn't just be a continuous market. It should be the melding of a call market together with the continuous market. I've got a suggestion: E-bay should offer call markets. We could just tell E-bay, "at 10:30 on March 22nd, we're going to trade IBM. People start putting in their prices and then we'll clear the market." I am sure E-bay could figure it out. It isn't that hard.

SIRRI: A number of you mentioned volatility, so let me unmuzzle myself for a minute. I figured we'd be talking about volatility, and we need to be very precise when we talk about it, so I ran a couple of numbers before I came up. For instance, the statement that the market is more volatile today than it has been in the past is inaccurate. If you look at the S&P 500 as a market, it is not more volatile. Not by conventional measures, not by the extreme points within the day. I ran those numbers for the past five or six years, and it is not more volatile.

Now, you do not make markets in the S&P 500, you make markets in individual names. I understand that very well. But, we've got to be careful because a couple of things have changed at once. We've seen the coming to market of a lot of firms that have no revenues and few tangible assets. If we gave you all the annual reports and asked each of you to write down your valuations, there would be a tremendous spread in the valuation.

It shouldn't be surprising that there is volatility when all of you enter the market to trade shares. That volatility is not due to the order handling rules. At the same time, you have new entrants into the market. One of the things that you have all said is that spreads declined. Sure, different people have been trading. We shouldn't be very surprised by that. When commissions came down, the price of trading came down. And when the price comes down for people, they are going to do more of it. That is, individuals are going to trade more today than they did in the past because it's cheaper to trade. Our structural arrangements weren't set up to handle that influx of individual traders.

Buzzy Geduld gave a good example. Buzzy, you were, in a sense, free riding on the quote. You were guaranteeing 5,000 up for a price that wasn't with mom and pop always coming in. Now mom and pop can come in, and you can't write that liability, you can't write that spread, because it gets too expensive. I don't debate that it got too expensive for you to do so. I don't know, though, what the right reaction should be. Should mom and pop not be able to come in?

GEDULD: The issue of volatility is complex. But to say the order handling rules had no part in it is incorrect. First of all, you just have to look at the landscape and see the number of firms that have dropped stocks. They didn't want to commit capital because the stocks were no longer profitable. Every time someone drops a stock and you have one less market maker, market depth is reduced.

Second, the real phenomenon about volatility that we haven't even touched yet, is the Internet broker and the Internet client. And through technology, everybody has the same information at the very same moment in time, and everybody wants to do the same thing at the same time. If you could look at one of our automated systems, at any point in time when there is news out, you would see something like five, ten, fifteen, 20,000 orders all lined up and queued to buy or sell the same stock at the same moment in time. It is the Internet player -- I'm not saying this is good or bad – that has created a lot of this volatility.

HARTS: Erik Sirri pointed out the possibility that the volatility of the S&P 500 hasn't increased that much. But I would guess that the stocks where volatility has exploded are those that trade on the new ATSs. For whatever reason, there is an attraction there.

SIRRI: I think that's right. There's a natural coincidence there because they tend to be technology-oriented companies, and the individuals that like to trade them are technology-users. But since they're mostly IPOs, they're also relatively small market cap. The dollar value of those stocks is still relatively small compared to the 13 trillion dollars of total market cap that we have in this country.

CORMACK: Didn't we experience a lot of the same occurrences in the '80s with bio techs? I've probably been in the business less than anyone on the panel; six years. But I've looked at some studies that show that there is a lot of individual stock volatility now via the Internet, but historically we've seen this in other groups at other times.

GEDULD: Bio techs don't even scratch the surface when you see what goes on in these Internet stocks. It's not even close.

SCHWARTZ: Volatility is key to all of this. But I want to add another dimension to the discussion. If you come to market with a share order that is 50% of average daily trading volume, how long does it take for that order to be worked off these days compared to in the recent past? Is this part of the volatility story?

PARCESEPE: May I attempt to answer that? In a word, "yes." It does take an extended period of time to execute a large order, and the process of breaking up an order for execution over time does accentuate volatility.

I have something else to say. The first thing you look at about volatility is cause and effect in the marketplace. When you have an order, whether you are representing Mike Cormack or anybody else, you have to decide what is the cause and effect, and that has a direct correlation to the day traders. By the way, the day traders on the New York are not the same as day traders on Nasdaq, because the day traders on Nasdaq got through SOES[39] and have a big advantage. Therefore, it kind of feeds on itself. So the minute you move, you now have to change the decision making process that you made two seconds ago, and react to that, which is the participation that we are excluded from because now our quote is on automatic. So it just feeds on itself.

I wanted to ask Mike, since he does both listed and over-the-counter, what is the day trading impact on the New York versus the over-the-counter?

CORMACK: It's all done by one person down there on the New York.

PARCESEPE: Do you believe that the over-the-counter is more, or less, or is it equal?

CORMACK: Without having any evidence, my guess would be that there is more day trading going on in the over-the-counter world, because of what Erik Sirri mentioned; the allure of the stocks. The day traders like the volatility.

PARCESEPE: But you don't think the fact that they could get in and out based on the dysfunctionality of the Nasdaq, causes the volatility?

CORMACK: Well, getting out of illiquid stocks in New York is not always easy, even for a small day trader. I have numerous examples of illiquid stocks that are quoted 200 shares up, a quarter point spread, and if you send a Dot order down there, even for 200 shares, there's no guarantee you will get it done at a quarter.

The same issues extend to New York that exist in Nasdaq. Frankly, I prefer to trade stocks in Nasdaq rather than in New York because I get a consistent treatment there. I may not always like my execution in Nasdaq, but at least I understand how it operates and I always get consistent treatment

[39] The Small Order Execution System (SOES) is an automatic execution system for orders up to 1,000 shares. SOES was developed by Nasdaq to ensure that small orders will be automatically executed at the best displayed price by directing the order to a Market Maker with the best bid price. It is mandatory for all Market Makers to participate in SOES for Nasdaq National Market securities.

there. In New York, I never know. Sometimes that quarter bid is good for 25, sometimes it's good for nothing. That is the frustration we deal with in both marketplaces.

MURPHY: I agree. I snuck into a couple of Internet trading rooms just to see what they do in there. It's interesting because it's all technology driven and it's all over-the-counter. I never heard anybody talk about a listed stock. I would say 99% of it was technology stocks.

PARCESEPE: But Michael, what if we adopted something like a central location -- not any different from what an ECN provides? I'm not saying a limit order book. I'm saying a display mechanism where these ECNs or these day traders who go through an ECN would have to be stacked up. That is a functionality that would not allow them to impact and shoot ten of the market makers who are displaying 100 shares simply because they don't have the time or the personnel to follow everything, so you are moving everything in waves.

The proposal now at the SEC is to "make everything electronic." But that will only result in getting the next Pentium III chip and having computers go 90 miles an hour and there you go.[40]

MURPHY: That is the problem with technology changing so rapidly. Every time we make a change, it's outdated. And we continually make changes, so we have to be careful that we don't paint ourselves into a corner.

PARCESEPE: There was a negative impact after we proposed SOES, and in the twelve intervening years nobody has addressed it. We've ended up with this patchwork of a computer.

DAVIS: I think day trading is great. If day traders can look into a dealer market and discover trends, they should act on it. They are seeing an inefficiency in a market structure, they're acting on it, and that's terrific.

HOLLY STARK [From the Floor]: Aldo, I think your comment about the need for a central limit order book is fabulous. It was an idea that was shot down by the dealer community despite strong support from the institutional side. I think that's what we are doing right now, between the two MMIDs[41] at Nasdaq that has been proposed, and some of the other initiatives such as

[40] On January 10, 2001, the SEC approved Nasdaq's Super Montage, an electronic information display trade execution system. This was the proposal that Aldo Parcesepe was referring to.

[41] Market Maker Identifications (MMIDs).

collapsing SOES and SelectNet[42] into one system. But we are backing into it, and are going to end up with a defective central limit order book.

We trade a lot of small cap stocks, so dealers are not going to let me use their capital too much. There are a lot more off-board stops happening in Nasdaq stocks, especially if you are trying to buy or sell these things where they're only trading 200 shares at a clip. You can go into a broker/dealer and they will stop[43] you at a certain price, it doesn't show up anywhere, while they are amassing a position or getting out of a position. I'd be interested in hearing if you guys are seeing that more and more?

PARCESEPE: Regarding the proposed central limit order book, Nasdaq wanted to be the broker/dealer, and that was the problem. I do not want the operator of the system to be my competitor. That is why the limit order book was shot down.

STARK: I understand that it's problematic if the person who is regulating you, also controls the system. But my understanding of it was that Nasdaq was going to provide a facility.

PARCESEPE: We have a facility. I want the name on the back end of my competitor. I don't want Nasdaq's name because then he becomes the broker/dealer and I'm shut out of the marketplace.

STARK: But those concerns could have been worked out.

PARCESEPE: No, they couldn't have. Nasdaq insisted on that. That is why the community fought against it. It's our livelihood. They're not the broker/dealer, and they shouldn't be the broker/dealer, but they insisted on it, so that is why we revoked it.

STARK: Maybe we're getting close to that abyss that Dick Sylla was talking about before.

SIRRI: Greg?

GREG IP [From the Floor]: Are Nasdaq stocks more volatile than New York stocks? If so, is it because of the types of stocks or because of the market structure? Would Perot Systems have been more volatile if its IPO had been on Nasdaq instead of New York? If it is true that the Nasdaq market structure contributes to the volatility, would it be less so if we had no automatic execution on Nasdaq? Would New York stocks be more volatile if the specialist was not allowed to touch every order before it was executed?

[42] SelectNet is an automated Nasdaq market service that enables securities firms to route orders, negotiate terms, and execute trades in Nasdaq securities, eliminating the need for verbal contact between trading desks.

[43] Stopping refers to a practice of a broker guaranteeing a customer a price for a stock, but not executing the order immediately in the hopes of finding a better price.

PARCESEPE: When you have a system like Nasdaq that allows the bid and the offer to be totally different, especially in new issues where somebody bids two or three points above the offer, yes, I think you have a lot more volatility. And you have a lot more difficulty accepting the assumption that the market is going to find its own level.

It's a function of the market structure and not whether it's an auction or a negotiated market. I can't believe that anybody would support having a 97 bid while the stock is offered at 90.

SIRRI: Jay Peake?

PEAKE: The market is changing so rapidly you can't keep up with it. Yet, every time there is a release from the SEC, they give you six months to think about it and comment, then it takes another year to implement, then they get into all the details. If the SEC weren't writing these regulations on the micro management of markets, wouldn't you all be able to adapt better and quicker? Should the SEC lay off a bit and let the market decide, or should the regulators design the markets?

MURPHY: I don't think regulators are supposed to design the markets.

PEAKE: They are supposed to facilitate, though. It's been 25 years since the law was passed telling them to facilitate the development of a national market. Do we have a true national market system for equities today? Yes or no?

PARCESEPE: Twenty-five years ago they mandated the development of a national market system, but the computers that we have on our desks today have only been developed over the past four or five years. The evolutionary process is through the computerization. As Buzzy said, bringing value added liquidity to the marketplace by having a larger capital commitment is going to fuel that market, not dampen it. I am not happy about committing less money to the marketplace. It's a defensive mechanism. It's not something positive.

PEAKE: But in 1970 and 1971, when Nasdaq was developed, the dealers didn't want anything to do with changing the system to have more functionality. They wanted an electronic pink sheet. They wouldn't settle for anything else. I made a motion on the board to allow electronic execution of orders. I couldn't get a second for that motion. But it has cost the United States an awful lot because nowhere else in the world have they copied the New York Stock Exchange.

SIRRI: Let's return to Jay Peake's original question about the difference between the SEC's role and the market participant's role. I was wondering if anyone else has anything to say about that.

HARTS: I think the SEC definitely has a role to play. An example of that is ITS. The way ITS is designed, one exchange can nullify any change in ITS. ITS is, in my view, one step towards a true national market system. At the same time, anyone can kill any innovation. How are we going to get around that? To me, the only way is to have the SEC involved.

PEAKE: Or get rid of ITS.

HARTS: The SEC is well meaning, and has a lot of good ideas about reforming the national market system. But it often seems that whenever rule making gets down to the details, something always appears that changes the intent of the original proposal. For instance, this idea of having dual MMIDs for Nasdaq market makers. That really came about because of a loophole that was inserted in the ECN rule, which allowed an ECN to charge a commission when another participant hit the ECN's bid through SelectNet. You can make an argument for whether or not any market center participant should be allowed to charge a commission. An exchange specialist cannot charge a commission if you hit his bid. But what is striking is that Nasdaq market makers cannot charge when someone hits their bid, but ECNs can. I could never quite understand the intent of that rule provision. You have to be careful when you ask for the regulators' involvement. Sometimes you get what you wish for.

GEDULD: I think the regulators should protect the public and make sure we have a level playing field. But I don't think the regulators should be involved in structural change. Structural change should be developed through competition. There is enough competition in this country to take care of that.

SIRRI: Bill Harts, it seems to me that the scope of the firm might have changed. For instance, the businesses that a large integrated investment bank might be in, are changing. We've seen firms purchase trading venues and purchase ECNs. From your perspective, what do you see as the pluses and minuses of a firm like Salomon Smith Barney, buying up an ECN?

HARTS: We've been doing a lot of self-examination about that recently. As most people know, we are one of the participants in the Strike ECN, which has merged with the BRUT ECN. Clearly, we're not burying our heads in the sand. ECNs and ATSs are a brave new world. We intend to be part of it. Any firm that tries to ignore it, does so at their own risk. Most realize this is the way the landscape is going to look going forward. We might as well embrace it.

SIRRI: Would all of you agree with that?

MURPHY: It would be interesting to see if the buy-side firms do that.

SIRRI: Well, that's a good question, to the extent that the buy-side firms are ultimately the source of liquidity. One of the things that happened in the Nasdaq market was that some of the market makers got together and mutualized. They asked themselves why should they pay out when they can mutualize and capture it themselves. It's not that big a leap to realize that a buy-side firm will want the same thing.

MURPHY: We've talked for years about a coop-type of environment from the mutual fund or investment management side of the business. There is no reason to think that that couldn't happen at some point.

SIRRI: Wasn't that the idea behind Instinet? It was an institutional network.

HARTS: Yes it was.

SIRRI: As I remember from my financial history, the idea was who met who. Do any of you think there is a chance of that happening today?

MURPHY: Sure. We are now embracing technology to the point where people are just learning how to use it. There are a lot of things out there that are possible, that people don't want to talk about because they don't want to think it could happen, or they just haven't gotten to that point yet. But as the next generation comes forward, and as we become more comfortable with technology, things will develop more quickly.

SIRRI: We will now run down the panel for closing statements.

CORMACK: Buzzy or Aldo can also comment on this as we move down the line but, frankly, I get the impression that in many ways a lot of the best traders are the day traders. And the institutions are increasingly unwilling to make decisions. Whether it's because of volatility or because they're understaffed, I don't know. But we run into orders all the time now that are volume weighted average priced (VWAP), and this is the goal of that order throughout the day.

From my perspective, that is job threatening. Why am I here if we are just going to trade at VWAP? Why don't we just have a good call auction and get it done? It's very difficult for us to run into a situation where somebody is offering us 100,000 shares and grows that order into half a million. It is difficult just to trade it and get it done. What we find more and more is that institutions are less willing to make those pricing decisions during the day. It is frustrating for us because we feel like we are ready to. I'd be curious to hear from the sell-side whether or not that is a phenomenon that they see growing.

GEDULD: Smart institutions don't worry about the weighted average costs during the day. They are buying a stock because they want to own it, and they don't really care if it's up an eighth, up a quarter, or up a half. They are buying it for a long-term investment, not for an hour and a half, or a day and a half. So, I personally find that the institutions we do business with are not really worried about that.

CORMACK: You are not seeing an increase in those types of orders?

HARTS: We've seen an increase in those types of orders, but mainly from time zones where people are sleeping during our trading hours, like in the Far East.

PARCESEPE: Michael, maybe I do a different business than everybody else, but we've seen an increase in that. The reason is that people who want to get into Amazon.com or Yahoo and who have 100,000 or 200,000 shares to buy, are scared to pull the trigger because they are paranoid that the stock is going to fluctuate 10 or 20 points. So their decision-making process is, "I'm going to buy a small amount now, and see what happens." Throughout the day there is mediocrity, but it's a protective action. It is different than saying, "I know what I'm doing and I'm going to get into the marketplace, irregardless of where it closes."

GEDULD: The problem there is, if you give it all to Aldo Parcesepe, the stock moves 20 points. If you give it all to us, that doesn't happen.

PARCESEPE: Buzzy, then it's ten points, not 20.

MURPHY: We talk a lot about the day traders, but we forget sometimes that we have been in a phenomenal bull market and that some intriguing new companies have been going public. It will be interesting to see what happens to the day traders if the market ever pulls back for a year, or six to eight months. At some point it will. I always think about the guy who will have to tell his wife that he has lost his pension fund, or that he has lost the down payment on the house. What will happen in this business? Will it be as big in a year, or two years, or three years as it is today, or will it be in a different form? I'm not sure.

DAVIS: Just a comment about brokers getting involved in ECNs. They seem to be falling all over themselves to buy a piece of an ECN, or to get in on small order action. In a way, that is a good business decision. I think it's known as diversifying. In terms of market structure, they're wondering about the long run for a dealer market, and they want to be well positioned in an order-driven market. I can only suggest again to them that they also try to position themselves in call markets so that they really are diversified.

SIRRI: It's been a terrific discussion. I think it illustrates that the surest way to take the heat off of yourself is to let the industry participants chat amongst themselves.

CHAPTER 5: VIEW FROM NASDAQ

Alfred R. Berkeley, III

The topic of this book is the *Impact of Regulation on the Trading Markets.* In my chapter, I thought it might make sense to address some of the issues from a little different perspective. The advances in technology and communications, the growth of the Internet, and the proliferation of new companies that have developed these technologies and platforms have played a huge role in the creation of our new economy. These substantial achievements would not be possible without the industry's new regulatory reforms that are impacting significantly on the new investor class.

We at Nasdaq are perhaps in a better position than anyone to understand the impact of regulation in terms of trading and trade counts— and we are a far better market today because of the new regulatory landscape. As a result of these changes, there has been a marked increase in order display, that has had a dramatic impact on the quality of our market. Transparency has greatly increased, transaction costs have decreased, and liquidity has flourished. In addition, individual investors have improved access to the markets, while new market participants and market centers continue to flourish as well—all due to improved regulation of the markets.

Today, we have something that is the envy of the world—a trading market that is open and accessible to people from all walks of life. However, this hasn't always been the case. Just 50 years ago, a mere four percent of American households were actively involved in the equity markets—meaning they owned an equity directly, or owned equities in a mutual fund. By 1996, however, the market had grown to include 42 percent of American homes. Today, close to *half* of all American homes own equity in the markets. This is attributable largely to the low cost and easy accessibility to the markets by individual investors. This is an enormous democratization of the markets. As a result of this democratization, there's been a huge influx of investors into the markets—most notably, baby boomers and young adults, or Generation X.

In recent years, baby boomers have come to realize that social security alone will not be able to sustain them throughout their retirements. About two years ago, we conducted a survey that asked questions regarding financial planning for the future. Not surprisingly, the respondents replied that social security meant very little to them in terms of their current or anticipated standard of living. As a result, they have begun to invest in the equity markets—most often through mutual funds and in funds they manage directly.

Increasingly, another demographic group is taking advantage of this electronic, easy, cheap access—young adults, or Generation X. This group holds a few advantages over older investors—they are far more financially savvy than their parent's generation, and they have a great deal of previously unattainable investment information available at their fingertips. As a result, they understand and participate in the markets at a comparatively earlier age. However, American investors aren't the only players contributing to the reshaping of the trading markets. Investors of all ages and backgrounds *around the world* are participating increasingly in the markets as well, thanks to instant access to information and, specifically, the Internet.

It's very hard to talk about commerce or Wall Street these days without mentioning the presence and power of the Internet. Never before has so much information been able to reach so many people in so little time. It is the vehicle that has put the public's insatiable demand for immediate access to information in the fast lane and has dramatically altered the way business is being conducted all over the world. More and more people are relying on the Internet for accurate, timely, financial information as well as an invaluable investing tool. From where we stand, one of the most telling measures of this is the dramatic increase in page views of our flagship Web site and the remarkable explosion in Nasdaq volume.

For example, online trading grew from 17 percent to 25 percent in 1999, and trading volume itself increased substantially during that time as well. At the same time, online and discount brokerages grew at 88 percent and 78 percent, respectively. These are staggeringly large numbers for any business. It is important to understand that these numbers do not necessarily represent business that is being taken away from traditional wire houses. The market has simply grown. At the market level, physical exchanges are being challenged by the increasing strength of the computer network—an interesting shift in power.

You could look at the integrated firms as containing both the order gathering and the order execution capability. Wholesalers in conjunction with the electronic firms specialize in different functions of the market and work together to create a powerful business model. As a result of this shift in power, we're seeing a marked increase in wholesaler volume. As this increased growth comes into Nasdaq, there is a dramatic shift in dollar volume towards the electronic, modern, cheap accessible model that we have.

This new shift in power— in conjunction with the creation of innovative technology— has contributed significantly to the regulatory reforms that we are seeing today. We are sorting out the most efficient way to reapportion costs to make these regulatory changes have sound economic fundamentals, to make them stand on their own legs. This will mean taking the cross subsidies out of our pricing that pay for regulation, then figuring out the most effective way to make explicit the costs of regulation. These costs have been bundled in because regulation is not an expense anyone wants to pay for explicitly.

In fact, regulation has been paid for disproportionately by the 20 percent of the firms that do 80 percent of the trades. These are 50 to 60 firms out of about 2,000 NASD member firms that may not even participate as Market Makers, but as order entry firms. As a result, there are two tiers of subsidization. There are large Market Makers generally subsidizing order entry firms, and we're working diligently to sort this situation out. We are also using quite a bit of sophisticated accounting to do the cost analysis to make this work while trying to figure out a pricing strategy that gives us the kind of ceilings on what we charge the large participants. This way, large participants will not be interested in leaving the network entirely, and yet we will not charge so much that small participants can't afford to be in the network.

Another issue we're examining is how we as an organization balance interests while mutualizing the technological improvements that come along. Unless we continue to invest in technological improvements and make them available mutually to everyone, we will have no economic function for being and people will inevitably drift other ways. We know some might say there's nothing wrong with that. It's perfectly okay if Nasdaq goes away. However, we think it is important to note that we are providing tremendous capability to handle significant surges in volume—a multi-hundred million dollar telecommunications contract with MCI to facilitate an 8-billion share day.

These are costs like AT&T incurred to create a national system of telephones in which AT&T was overcharging the business user and undercharging the rural farmer for telephony. We have whole sets of cross subsidies developed in the Nasdaq pricing structure now. We are being forced to look at unravelling these, because we now have new market entrants. These new competitors all want to have a time advantage for their participants. However, there is a public policy that says everyone should get fair and equal access to markets all around the country. We've been providing this equal access.

Back on the subject of technology, our recent technological initiatives—namely our proposed SuperMontage—will play a substantial role in this new regulatory environment. We believe the right model for the Nasdaq is a series of voluntary facilities that people can use or choose not to use. The markets can sort out whether or not this is a facility that the market wants. The SuperMontage will be an important step in achieving greater centrality and less fragmentation in the marketplace, while allowing competition to flourish. In essence, it will encourage innovation and competition, improve transparency and liquidity, and provide numerous benefits to the individual investor—another result of the regulatory reforms.

Clearly, we are a far better market today as a result of industry regulatory reform. Our growth and structural changes have resulted in a flourishing market that remains the envy of the world. Investors will continue to see a marked increase in services as we continue to invest in technology. We will continue to invite more competition on a level playing field. As we move to the future, we will continue to build upon the new investor friendly, well-regulated market environment. And we will continue to flourish as the pre-eminent market of the future.

CHAPTER 6: VIEW FROM THE SEC-PROMOTING FAIR AND EFFICIENT MARKETS AS A REGULATORY END

Laura Simone Unger[44]

Since this conference focuses on regulation, I thought I would indulge in a brief philosophical discussion about what considerations factor into the Securities and Exchange Commission's ("Commission") rulemaking process. Although the Commission has one overarching mission -- investor protection -- it must also promote fair and efficient markets.[45]

When a rulemaking or some other matter comes before the Commission, however, the analysis usually focuses more on addressing investor protection concerns, particularly when the rulemaking or matter is controversial. Rarely, and then usually only as an afterthought, does the staff or a Commissioner add as a justification that the rulemaking "promotes fair and efficient markets."

Why is this? I can think of at least a couple of reasons.

For one, investor protection has a great deal of populist appeal. Announcing that we're doing something because it promotes fair and efficient markets has no such appeal. At best it appears coldly technocratic. After all, how could a regulatory agency side with Wall Street against Main Street?

Second, protecting investors requires the Commission to take an affirmative act -- generally noticed -- by layering on another level of regulation. On the other hand, promoting fair and efficient markets may

[44] Ms. Unger has served as a Commissioner of the U.S. Securities and Exchange Commission since November 1997. Before that, Ms. Unger served as Counsel to the U.S. Senate Committee on Banking, Housing, and Urban Affairs. The Commission, as a matter of policy, disclaims responsibility for any private publication or statement by its officials. The views expressed in this article are solely those of the author and do not necessarily reflect the views of the Commission, other Commissioners, or the Commission staff. Ms. Unger would like to thank Jon Kroeper, Counsel to the Commissioner, for his assistance in the preparation of this chapter.

[45] Section 106 of the National Securities Market Improvement Act of 1996 requires the Commission to consider efficiency, competition, and capital formation in its "public interest" standard analysis. PL 104-290, 110 Stat. 3416, 3424-25 (1996) (codified in 15 U.S.C. 78s(b)(6)).

require the Commission to refrain from imposing regulation -- generally unnoticed.

Finally, it is a lot more difficult -- possibly technocratic once more -- to quantify the benefits of promoting fair and efficient markets. So the Commission may more easily rationalize its actions by pointing to the goal of investor protection.

Obviously the competing interests of investor protection and fair and efficient markets are not entirely mutually exclusive. Consider the implications of forgoing investor protection in favor of the markets. How attractive would the markets be to investors? Piling on too much regulation, however, may overly protect investors to the detriment of the marketplace. Do investors really benefit under that scenario either?

What I am saying is that the Commission should not lose sight of the markets in its attempts to protect investors. We need both -- investors are important to the market and the market is important to investors. Promoting fair and efficient markets is a *sine qua non* to achieving investor protection. But it is more than that -- it is critical to the global economy, the nation's capital-raising process, and the securities industry generally.

Now that I have emphasized the importance of promoting fair and efficient markets, I will touch on how the Commission actually undertakes this obligation in the context of the equity markets.

First, I will talk about the underpinnings of the principles that guide our regulation of the equities markets. Then, I will explain from my perspective how the Commission applied these principles in our recent rulemaking on alternative trading systems ("ATS") and exchanges.[46] Finally, I will look ahead and highlight future issues for the Commission that will come about from Regulation ATS and general market changes.

I. Principles Guiding U.S. Equity Market Regulation

The 1975 Act Amendments to the Securities Exchange Act of 1934 ("Exchange Act") lay the framework for the structure of our equities markets. As part of the 1975 Act Amendments, Congress added Section 11A to the Exchange Act, directing the Commission to facilitate the development of a National Market System ("NMS") for securities.[47]Section 11A sets forth the

[46] Exchange Act Release No. 40760 (December 8, 1998), 63 FR 70844 (ATS Adopting Release).

[47] 15 U.S.C. 78k-1. Congress did not dictate the structure of a NMS. Instead, Congress set out the goals for a NMS, which were to assure:

(i) economically efficient execution of securities transactions;

(ii) fair competition among brokers and dealers, among exchange markets, and between exchange markets and markets other than exchange markets;

three principles that have guided the Commission's regulation of the equity markets over the last quarter century: (1) creating linkages among the equity markets; (2) eliminating anti-competitive practices; and (3) promoting the use of technology to foster competition and innovation.

With the first principle, Congress believed that linkages among the markets trading NMS securities was a precondition to a NMS. As a result, Congress gave the Commission broad authority to create and oversee these linkages. The second principle reflects Congressional belief in maintaining a competitive playing field among NMS participants. To encourage fair competition, Congress charged the Commission with the continuing obligation both to assure the equivalent regulation of NMS participants and to review self-regulatory organization ("SRO") rules for anti-competitive impacts. The third principle reflects Congressional desire for the Commission to use technology to link the markets and promote innovation and competition in the NMS.[48]

II. Applying These Principles to the Regulation of Alternative Trading Systems

Unfortunately for me, but fortunately for you, I have not been given enough space to justify twenty-five years of regulatory policy. I am afraid you will have to take my word on it -- we have been very consistent. Instead, I will limit this discussion to current rulemaking and talk about how the three principles I just mentioned impacted the timing and content of Regulation ATS.

A. The 1980s: ATSs Begin to Mature

By the early 1980s, the basic linkages necessary for a NMS were in place. There was a consolidated quotation and transaction reporting system. The exchanges and -- with Commission intervention on the NASD's behalf -- the NASD participated in the Intermarket Trading System ("ITS"), an intermarket linkage for listed stocks with limited trade-through protection for participant

---

(iii) the availability to brokers, dealers, and investors of information with respect to quotations for and transactions in securities;

(iv) the practicability of brokers executing investors orders in the best market; and

(v) an opportunity, consistent with [(i) and (iv)], for investors' orders to be executed without the participation of a dealer.

15 U.S.C. 78k-1(a)(1)(C).

[48] This only underscored the Commission's longstanding support for the application of technology to the markets, which went back at least as far as our 1963 Special Study of Securities Markets. See Report of Special Study of Securities Markets, 88th Cong., 1st Sess., H.R. Doc. No. 95, pt 2 Ch.VI.J. & Ch.VII.E.

markets.[49] The Commission proposed, but refrained from enacting, any truly radical changes to the U.S. equity market structure, such as creating a consolidated public limit order book, mandating market-wide limit order priority, or requiring order-by-order routing to the market with the best price.[50] Although the Commission achieved the significant goal of creating the NMS mechanisms, they did not attract any substantial competition to the primary markets.[51]

ATSs remained an insignificant factor in the NMS well into the 1980s. Towards the end of that decade, however, they became increasingly popular for a number of reasons.[52] Most importantly, ATSs provided anonymity to their participants. Institutions could avoid information leakage by working their orders themselves on an ATS, rather than by using a market maker or block positioner. Moreover, because orders entered into ATSs were not integrated into the public quote, an institution using an ATS could reduce the market impact costs incurred by exposing a large order publicly on an exchange or Nasdaq. The increased popularity of ATSs among institutions fuelled market makers' and specialists' interests. They began to access ATSs as a source of liquidity, a place to anonymously put orders priced better than the NBBO,[53] and trade with other participants' orders at such improved prices.[54]

[49] Exchange Act Rel. No. 19456 (Jan. 27, 1983), 48 FR 4938 (order authorizing operation of ITS on an indefinite basis); Exchange Act Rel. No. 18713 (May 6, 1982), 47 FR 20413 (order amending ITS Plan to include the NASD as a participant). The Nasdaq Stock Market ("Nasdaq") serves as the *de facto* intermarket linkage for Nasdaq National Market and SmallCap securities.

[50] Exchange Act Rel. No. 14416 (January 26, 1978), 43 FR 4354; Exchange Act Rel. No. 15671 (March 22, 1979), 44 FR 20360.

[51] See, e.g., NYSE, FACT BOOK 1990 (1990) at 22-23 (comparing NYSE, regional exchange, and NASD third market maker Consolidated Tape share and trade volume in NYSE-listed stocks, 1980-1990). But see Division of Market Regulation, SEC, Market 2000: An Examination of Current Equity Market Developments (January 1994) (Market 2000 Study) at II-10 (asserting that "although the regional exchanges may not provide vigorous quote competition to the NYSE, they have provided meaningful and needed service competition .... [and] vigorous cost competition through lower transaction fees and have developed new products.").

[52] See, e.g., NYSE, FACT BOOK 1995 (1995) at 25-26 (comparing NYSE and Instinet reported Consolidated Tape volume in NYSE-listed stocks, 1985-1990).

[53] National Best Bid or Offer (NBBO) refers to the single highest bid price from among all bids quoted by the various participants (stock exchange specialists and third market dealers) in the Consolidated Quotation Service and the single lowest offer price from among all offers quoted by those participants.

Also important, the technology used by ATSs had matured to the point where it was dependable and cost-effective. Finally, registered as broker-dealers and not as exchanges, ATSs became nimble competitors, able to rapidly offer new services to their subscribers without the need to wait for regulatory approval.[55]

B. 1989: Reasons Why ATS Regulation Was Premature - Rule 15c2-10

In 1989, faced with the steady growth of ATS trading volumes the Commission dusted off and re-proposed the decades old Rule 15c2-10.[56] Originally proposed in 1969, the rule was intended to respond to the regulatory challenge posed by Instinet and other forerunners of today's ATSs. At that time, the Commission found it difficult to fit ATSs into either the exchange or broker-dealer category.[57] Rule 15c2-10 would have imposed exchange-like regulation on ATSs serving market functions.[58] Although I

---

[54] See Exchange Act Rel. No. 37619A (September 6, 1996), 61 FR 48290 (Order Handling Rules Adopting Release).

[55] By way of contrast, any significant new service offered by the exchanges or the NASD is treated as a proposed rule change, and is subject to the notice and comment requirements of the Exchange Act, and approval by Commission order. 15 U.S.C. 78s(b). But see infra note 67 and accompanying text (describing Rule 19b-5 pilot trading program exemption).

[56] Exchange Act Rel. No. 26708 (April 18, 1989), 54 FR 15429 (Rule 15c2-10 Reproposing Release).

[57] Exchange Act Rel. No. 8661 (August 4, 1969), 34 FR 12952 (Rule 15c2-10 Proposing Release). The Commission withdrew the original 15c2-10 proposal in 1975 as no longer necessary in light of the regulatory scheme provided for in the 1975 Amendments. See Exchange Act Rel. No. 11673 (September 23, 1975), 40 FR 45422.

[58] Rule 15c2-10 would have required an ATS (then called a proprietary trading system ("PTS") to submit a plan regarding the operation of the system to the Commission. Specifically, the Commission would publish the plan for a 120 day minimum notice and comment period and approve it if the plan met certain standards. The plan would have to include a description of the system's operation; procedures for providing or denying access to the system; requirements for ensuring financial soundness of participants; procedures for complying with the terms and conditions of the plan; procedures for dealing with operational failure; agreements to preserve certain trading records, reporting possible violations by participants, and supervising participants' activities for possible securities law violations; procedures to safeguard funds; and agreements to permit Commission and SRO inspections. The Commission could impose any terms and conditions upon the approval of a plan that it deemed appropriate to protect investors, maintain fair and orderly markets, and perfect the mechanism of a NMS. In addition, the Commission would treat proposed amendments to a plan in a similar fashion as proposed rule changes submitted by exchanges under Section

was not there at the time, the Commission prudently exercised regulatory restraint, resisting the impulse to adopt what would have been a premature and overly burdensome regulatory scheme.

But why allow ATSs to operate largely outside the regulatory framework for exchanges? One reason, despite their tremendous growth, was that ATSs still comprised a relatively small part of trading in the NMS.[59] Regulating them like exchanges would have provided few benefits to the markets, while placing substantial burdens on the still-nascent ATSs.

Moreover, the Commission wanted to encourage the growth of ATSs as a source of significant potential competition for the primary markets. In the spirit of nurturing technological innovation and competition, the Commission instead imposed a quarterly reporting requirement on ATSs by adopting Rule 17a-23.[60] The quarterly reporting provided the Commission with data on ATSs, to allow for a better understanding of their operations, and providing a sounder basis for any future regulation.

C. 1997: Reasons Why Time Was Ripe for an ATS Regulatory Scheme

By 1997, ATSs comprised at least 20% of the volume of Nasdaq securities and around four percent of listed volume.[61] The Commission's Order Handling Rules, implemented in 1997, were the first step in bringing ATSs into the NMS. The Order Handling Rules amended the Quote Rule to

---

19(b) of the Act. Moreover, the Commission could exempt an ATS from any requirements of Rule 15c2-10. See Rule 15c2-10 Reproposing Release, supra note 56.

Under the original Rule 15c2-10 proposal, the Commission would approve ATS plan and plan amendments (although without an opportunity for public notice and comment) under similar standards as the reproposal, and subject to any terms and conditions the Commission saw fit to impose. However, the explicit requirements for a plan were limited to: rules of operation designed to prevent the system from disseminating misleading information and to prevent manipulative or fraudulent misuse of the system; a description of system architecture and integrity and security standards; and provisions for preserving and retrieving records and Commission access to such information. See Rule 15c2-10 Proposing Release, supra note 57.

[59] In 1991, the total share volume on ATSs was 2.9 billion shares. In 1992, it had grown to 4.9 billion shares. For the first half of 1993, it was 4.7 billion shares (of which 87% was in Nasdaq stocks and 13% was in listed stocks). During this same period, ATSs captured 13% of the volume in Nasdaq NM Securities volume and 1.4% of NYSE-listed volume. Exchange Act Rel. No. 35124 (December 28, 1994), 59 FR 66702 at n.18 (citing Market 2000 Study at II-12 and 13.)

[60] Exchange Act Rel. No. 35124 (December 28, 1994), 59 FR 66702.

[61] Exchange Act. Rel. No. 38672 (May 23, 1997), 62 FR 30485 (Exchange Concept Release).

incorporate the best-priced market maker and specialist orders from ATSs into the public quote stream. The Rules also required ATSs to give non-participants access to these orders on the same terms as system participants.[62]

The Order Handling Rules did not complete the job of fully integrating ATSs' orders into the NMS, however, since a significant percentage of the best-priced orders in ATSs remained outside of the NMS, available only to ATS subscribers.[63] At the time, the Commission also regulated ATSs mostly on an *ad hoc* basis, by issuing "exchange" and "compliant ECN" no-action letters. Not surprisingly, this *ad hoc* approach did not provide the coherent regulatory scheme needed to guide the future growth of ATSs.

Moreover, given their emergence as full-blown competitors to traditional exchanges, the regulatory disparities between ATSs and exchanges had become more pronounced. Traditional exchanges and Nasdaq saw themselves disadvantaged *vis-à-vis* ATSs. The Exchange Act imposed a business model on the exchanges and Nasdaq that made even internal approval of changes to their trading systems a significant undertaking. And of course, the changes still needed Commission approval after that.

Up to this point, the Commission's only regulatory arsenal to deal with ATSs was the blunt tool of an exchange model. As the experience with Rule 15c2-10 showed, the Commission was concerned about stifling competition and therefore unwilling to impose this exchange-type regulation on ATSs.

The Commission could have enlisted Congress's help in the form of legislation -- with unpredictable results. Ultimately, Congress did in fact provide critical assistance by adding exemptive authority to the Exchange Act in the National Securities Markets Improvement Act of 1996. This exemptive authority gave the Commission the means to craft an appropriate regulatory scheme for ATSs[64] -- one that incorporates them into the existing market structure without stifling innovation and competition.

D. 1998: Regulation ATS and the Underlying Equity Market Regulatory Structure

Regulation ATS embodies the Commission's three regulatory principles contained in Section 11A: (1) it improves market linkages and transparency,

[62] See Order Handling Rules Adopting Release, supra note 54 (discussion on amendments to the Quote Rule, 17 C.F.R. 240.11Aa3-1).

[63] In the ATS Adopting Release, the Commission noted that approximately 94 percent of non-market maker broker-dealer and institutional orders in ATSs that could have improved the NBBO were not in the public quote stream. See ATS Adopting Release, supra note 46, at 192.

[64] 15 U.S.C. 78mm.

(2) it equalizes competition, and (3) it encourages competition through technological innovation.

First, Regulation ATS improves market linkages by requiring ATSs to become SRO members, thus integrating their trading interest more closely into an existing market.

Second, Regulation ATS improves market transparency by making all the best prices for the significant markets in any equity security available in the NMS. ATSs with more than five percent of the trading volume in any security must make <u>all</u> of their best-priced orders in those securities available to the public quote stream and accessible to non-subscribers.

This aspect of Regulation ATS illustrates my point that sometimes the benefits of investor protection (*i.e.*, price transparency), may be outweighed by the regulatory and competitive burdens that such a mandate may impose on the markets. While I support the concept of encouraging the markets to provide as much pre-trade price transparency as possible -- I do not believe that this end should be pursued at any cost. Instead, the Commission generally should rely on competition and investor choice to bring the optimal level of pre-trade transparency. Most ATSs have an open limit order book, pressuring exchanges to adopt the ATS standard by opening up their books more widely. The Commission should consider mandating a minimum level of transparency only in situations like the Limit Order Display Rule, where anti-competitive practices undermined the integrity of the public quote and the efficiency of the markets to the detriment of market participants.

The timing of the institutional display requirement also gave me pause. The Order Handling Rules wrought significant changes to market structure, some of which are still being worked out.[65] I am concerned about following so quickly on its heels with a requirement that might significantly impact institutional trading behaviour.

In spite of these concerns, I voted for Regulation ATS for two reasons. The Commission agreed to phase-in the institutional display requirement[66]

[65] Indeed, Nasdaq has continued to search for a market structure that is acceptable to its various constituencies in this new environment. <u>See</u>, <u>e.g.</u>, Exchange Act Rel. Nos. 36548 (December 1, 1995), 60 FR 63092 (Naqcess proposal); 39718 (March 4, 1998), 63 FR 12124 (integrated order delivery and execution system proposal); 41296 (April 22, 1999), 64 FR 19844 (proposal to modify SOES and SelectNet; reopening of comment period on central limit order file); and 41343 (May 6, 1999), 64 FR 24430 (Agency Quote proposal).

[66] Exchange Act Rel. No. 41297 (April 16, 1999), 64 FR 19450. High-volume ATSs must comply with the display requirement for 50 selected Nasdaq securities on August 23, 1999; 50% of all Nasdaq securities on September 28, 1999; 75% of all Nasdaq securities on April 25, 1999; and 100% of all Nasdaq securities on June 20, 2000. Moreover, ATSs will not

and overall, it improves the regulatory scheme -- at least in the context of today's market structure.

To return to the third of the regulatory principles, Regulation ATS equalizes competition by creating a more level playing field between ATSs and exchanges. The Commission clarified that the Exchange Act can accommodate for-profit exchanges, clearing the way for both existing exchanges to demutualize and ATSs to register as exchanges. If an exchange preferred the ATS business model, it could de-register as an exchange and comply with Regulation ATS. The Commission also adopted Rule 19b-5, which allows exchanges to operate pilot trading programs for up to two years without seeking Commission approval.[67] Rule 19b-5 is intended to reduce the regulatory disparity between exchanges and ATSs in starting up new trading systems.

Finally, Regulation ATS encourages competition through technological innovation. It doesn't take much to register as an ATS. An ATS must submit and keep current a Form ATS; register as a broker-dealer; become a member of a SRO; permit Commission and SRO inspections; maintain certain trading records; ensure the protection of subscribers' confidential trading information; and refrain from calling itself an "exchange" or "stock market."[68] None of the commenters on Regulation ATS raised any significant problems about complying with these requirements. The other requirements -- order display and access; fair access; capacity, security, and integrity standards -- only apply to high-volume ATSs.[69]

Accordingly, Regulation ATS allows new competitors to take advantage of technological developments without being overly burdened by regulation. Once ATSs become significant competitors in the NMS, of course -- all bets are off.

III. Future Developments

I will conclude by briefly mentioning some issues that each merit an entire article -- but I mention them mainly to pique your interest and to let you know what may attract the Commission's attention in the future. At the very least, they are on this Commissioner's list.

---

have to comply with the requirement with respect to exchange-listed securities until a mechanism is developed for the display of such securities.

[67] 17 C.F.R. 240.19b-5.

[68] See 17 CFR 242.301(b).

[69] See 17 CFR 242.301(b)(3), (b)(5) and (b)(6).

For-Profit SROs

In the ATS Adopting Release, the Commission made clear that national securities exchanges could adopt proprietary structures. Both the NYSE and the NASD are studying whether to demutualize and restructure themselves as for-profit organizations.

The International Securities Exchange, the Island ECN, and the Archipelago ECN already have filed applications to register as exchanges with for-profit structures. Among other issues, the Commission must closely evaluate whether a for-profit national securities exchange or association can adequately carry out its self-regulatory responsibilities under the Exchange Act.

Would a for-profit model place unacceptable pressures on the allocation of the resources necessary to perform self-regulation? Or, would a for-profit model actually incentivize full funding of self-regulatory obligations, since the value of a for-profit exchange necessarily includes maintaining the integrity of its market?

As part of its evaluation, the Commission may have to give consideration to formally separating exchanges' trading and self-regulatory functions and establishing a single self-regulatory organization. How would such an entity be funded? Could it achieve the purported benefits of self-regulation?

Conflicts between ATSs and Their SROs.

By tying member ATSs closer to the SRO that regulates them, Regulation ATS may heighten the conflict of interest for a SRO that operates a competing trading system. While we made clear in the ATS Adopting Release that we will exercise our oversight responsibility to minimize such conflicts, it will require a great deal of vigilance on our part going forward.[70]

We also will have to keep the exchange registration option a viable one for ATSs as a possible solution to this conflict of interest. Let me make clear, however, that registering as an exchange and becoming a SRO will be a significant undertaking, not for the faint of heart.

ATS Access Fees.

Regulation ATS basically left this difficult question open for another day. As you know, the Commission never wants to be a rate maker. Of course my own hope is that the markets will provide an equitable solution to the problem. Implicit and explicit pricing of access fees are two possible solutions.

[70] An example of this conflict is the concern that several ATSs have expressed with respect to the NASD's Super Montage proposal. See Exchange Act Release No. 42166 (November 22, 1999), 64 FR 69125 (December 6, 1999).

Indications of Interest.

The distinction between "orders" and "indications of interest" is an important one in considering whether a system is or is not an exchange.[71] The Commission will have to closely monitor systems that purport to merely display indications of interest to make sure they are not really functioning as exchanges.

Access by ATSs to ITS.

ATSs currently account for approximately 30% of Nasdaq volume, but have not been able to capture a significant portion of the volume in listed securities. Indeed, they have been limited to about four percent of listed volume for several years now. The likely reason for this is their lack of access to the public quote and the listed markets via ITS.

In the ATS Adopting Release, we encouraged the exchanges and the NASD to move promptly to establish such access. I had thought that the ITS Participants would act reasonably to avoid the Commission mandating such a linkage, but I grow less convinced about the prospect as time passes.[72]

ITS as an Intermarket Linkage.

Speaking more generally about ITS, I believe that the Commission needs to closely evaluate whether today's ITS should be the intermarket linkage to take us into the next millennium. An inappropriate linkage could impede the natural evolution of market structure. Does ITS provide a sufficient intermarket linkage considering market changes in the last twenty plus years since it was created and that most or all new entrants will be fully electronic markets?

Does ITS' governance structure -- with each participant having absolute veto power over proposed amendments to the ITS Plan -- have an anti-competitive impact on new entrants and current participants that want to adopt innovative trading facilities? Over a year ago, the Commission proposed rulemaking to amend the ITS Plan and replace the unanimous voting provision with a two-thirds majority requirement.[73] Should the Commission

[71] See ATS Adopting Release, supra note 46, at 21-24.

[72] In July 1998, the Commission proposed rulemaking to amend the ITS Plan to expand the link between ITS and the NASD's Computer Assisted Execution System ("CAES") link to include all exchange-listed securities (it currently is limited to securities continuously listed on an exchange after April 1980). CQS market makers (i.e., NASD-registered third market makers) would thereafter have ITS access equivalent to that of exchange specialists. The Commission solicited comment on whether NASD rules needed to be amended to allow ATSs to participate in CAES and the ITS/CAES linkage. Exchange Act Rel. No. 40260 (July 24, 1998), 63 FR 40748.

[73] Id.

act on this amendment, or is a more far-reaching reworking of ITS' governance structure necessary?

Trading Restrictions.

A number of rules restrict trading by one group of market participants or another in NMS securities. The principal ones that come to mind are off-board-trading restrictions, such as NYSE Rule 390. In 1980, the Commission adopted Rule 19c-3 to maintain the status quo until it could decide whether or not to abolish off-board-trading restrictions completely.[74] That was almost twenty years ago. Do off-board-trading restrictions serve a legitimate purpose today?[75]

At the very least, should the Commission consider lifting the restrictions for trading after the close of the primary trading session -- as our Division of Market Regulation recommended in its *Market 2000 Study* back in 1994?[76]

---

[74] Exchange Act Rel. No. 16888 (June 11, 1980), 45 FR 41125.

[75] The NYSE voted to rescind Rule 390 in December 1999. The Commission approved the NYSE's proposed rule change to rescind Rule 390 on May 5, 2000. See Exchange Act Release No. 42758, 65 FR 30175 (May 10,2000). There are two other provisions restricting trading among markets that come to mind. The first is the OTC-UTP Plan, which limits the number of OTC stocks that a national securities exchange can trade on an UTP basis. See Exchange Act Rel. No. 40896 (January 12, 1999) 64 FR 1834 (describing the Joint Transaction Reporting Plan for the National Market Securities Traded on an Exchange on an Unlisted or Listed Basis). The Chicago Stock Exchange recently received permission to increase the number of OTC stocks it could trade from 500 to 1000. Exchange Act Rel. No. 41392 (May 12, 1999), 64 FR 27839. However, the OTC-UTP Plan does not cover Nasdaq SmallCap securities. Accordingly, an exchange presently could not trade a SmallCap security UTP.

The second is Rule 12f-2 under the Exchange Act, which limits exchange, but not OTC, trading on the first day of an IPO to the exchange that listed the IPO. 17 C.F.R. 240.12f-2. In 1998, the regional exchanges recently filed a rulemaking petition with the Commission seeking to remove this restriction. On December 9, 1999, the Commission proposed a change to Rule 12f-2, permitting a national securities exchange to begin trading in an IPO issue pursuant to UTP immediately after the first trade in the security is reported by the listing exchange to the Consolidated Tape. See Exchange Act Release No. 42209, 64 FR 69975 (December 15, 1999). The Commission adopted this rule change on August 29, 2000. See Exchange Act Release No. 43217, 65 FR 53560 (September 5, 2000).

[76] Market 2000 Study, supra note 51, at III-9 to III-10. On October 13, 1999, the Commission approved certain SRO rule filings allowing for the implementation of an extended hours trading session on a pilot basis. See Exchange Act Release Nos. 42003 (October 13, 1999), 64 FR 56554 (October 20, 1999) (NASD-99-57); 42004 (October 13, 1999), 64 FR 56548 (October 20, 1999) (CHX-99-16).

Market Data Review.

As you may be aware, the Commission is presently reviewing the fee structure for market data and the role of data revenue in the operation of the markets. The markets have changed since the current structure was set up. Online investing in particular allows for the broad dissemination of real-time data. Given the huge volume of investor and other demand for this data, the time has come for the Commission to determine whether it is meeting its statutory responsibility to ensure that quote and trade information is available on terms that are "fair and reasonable" and "not unreasonably discriminatory."[77]

Options Market Review.

Although technically outside the scope of this Baruch Conference, I thought I would make a passing reference to the Commission's ongoing review of the options markets. The 1975 Act Amendments gave the Commission the ability to decide whether certain classes of securities were ripe for inclusion in the NMS.[78] While there is a consolidated quotation and trade reporting system, in many respects the options markets today resemble the equity markets in 1975. The options markets lack an intermarket linkage and trade-through protection. Moreover, neither the Firm Quote Rule nor the Limit Order Display Rule apply to options. We need to ask whether the options markets have matured sufficiently to implement the NMS mechanisms and rules applicable to the equities markets.

Conclusion

Given the pace of change today, the ink is barely dry on Regulation ATS and already I wonder how long this regulatory scheme will work. I do take solace in the fact that whatever the future market developments bring, the Commission will always be able to look to the guiding principles of regulation adopted in 1975. I'd be happy to answer any questions.

Discussion

STEIL: I want to ask you about the policy on direct access for foreign exchanges in the United States. My understanding is that at the moment the only foreign exchange for which the SEC is prepared to consider direct access

[77] 15 U.S.C. 78k-1(c)(1)(C) and (1)(D).

[78] 15 U.S.C. 78k-1(a)(2).

rights is Tradepoint.[79] Tradepoint is a very small United Kingdom exchange that accounts for less than half a percent of total share volume on the London Stock Exchange. It's also teetering on the edge of financial viability.

You emphasized at the outset that your primary mission was investor protection. Yet, the primary criterion you are using to decide whether foreign exchanges can have direct access into the U.S., is whether they have sufficiently low volume. In other words, if traders don't like to use these markets, if they are illiquid, you will allow them direct access into the U.S. On the other hand, if they're highly successful, highly liquid, and if investors abroad have confidence in them, then you will not allow them access to U.S. investors. This to me makes no sense, whatsoever.

The second part of my question ....

UNGER: That didn't sound like a question.

STEIL: Well, you could explain to me why I'm misunderstanding the situation.

UNGER: Where is the question mark?

STEIL: The second part of that question has to do with the access that the London Stock Exchange already has in the United States. For example, it's perfectly possible and normal for a U.S. institutional investor to pick up a telephone, call a broker in London, and place an order on the London Stock Exchange. That is legal, you have no problem with that. A U.S. institutional investor could also place an order through an Instinet screen that goes directly into the SETS[80] system of the London Stock Exchange. My understanding is that you have no problem with that either.

If you have no problem with either of these things, why do you have a problem with the U.S. institutional investor putting an order directly onto SETS? That would save us, as investors in these mutual funds, enormous sums of money and unnecessary intermediation.

UNGER: I think what you are asking me is, why aren't we working harder to have a more global market?

STEIL: No.

UNGER: Or you are asking me specifically about those two instances? First, Tradepoint has not been signed off on yet by the entire Commission.[81]

[79] Instinet, leading a consortium of companies including Morgan Stanley Dean Witter, J.P. Morgan, American Century, Archipelago, and Warburg Dillon Read, acquired a 54.4% stake in Tradepoint on July 8, 1999.

[80] SETS, the Stock Exchange Electronic Trading Service, is the electronic order book trading system of the London Stock Exchange.

[81] Tradepoint received SEC approval on March 23, 1999.

STEIL: But I'm asking about the criteria that you use, not the final decision.

UNGER: I did look at Tradepoint. I saw the demonstration and I think it's a wonderful system. I wish we had a central limit order book the way they do. But I would assume that the reasoning is that it's an experiment, and we don't want to bring in something that has a huge market share right off the bat. That doesn't mean that we wouldn't change those criteria in the future. But I don't know the specifics. That's something that is done in the Division of Market Regulation. I didn't negotiate the agreement, but I did think it was a good thing to do. If it turns out that it is popular and successful, it may or may not be something that we get to review again. We need to take steps incrementally, and if this is an incremental step, it's better than no step at all.

With respect to your second question, I am not familiar enough with SETS to comment on it. I wish we had a more direct link into the other markets, and we do need a more global market. I was having a conversation with the new Chairman of SIA (Securities Industry Association) yesterday,[82] about why it costs so much money to register a company in each country, and why there isn't one set of standards. These are a couple of the many issues we need to look at on a global basis. We are just not there right now.

DAVIS: I was confused by your initial remark that most of your time is spent working on investor protection. I wonder if you can expand on what you mean by protection? My first thought was that you are talking about protection from fraud, but it seems like you mean protection as a rubric for getting into the things that you say you don't spend a whole lot of time on, like fair and efficient markets.

UNGER: I'm confused by your question.

DAVIS: How much of your time is spent on matters having to do with fraud, and how much is spent on other things that you put under that rubric of investor protection?

UNGER: I'll give you an example. As I discussed in the context of the institutional order display, if the idea is to obtain better market transparency for investor protection, is the burden of providing that information (which hasn't been provided before) worth the benefit of investors seeing that order reflected in the display?

DAVIS: I'm confused. That has nothing to do with fraud.

UNGER: No, but it's different in every rule making. In the context of Rule 15c2-11, it will prohibit brokers who quote a pink sheet stock from

[82] At the time of the conference, the SIA Chairman was James W. Brinkley, and the Chairman-Elect is Mark B. Sutton.

piggy-backing other quotes. They will have to obtain information about a company and verify that the quote makes sense.

DAVIS: Could you comment on the Commission's use of exemptive authority?[83]

UNGER: Congress had been thinking of exemptive authority in the context of company registration, which is a proposal that Commissioner Wallman was working on at the time. That was an example of how the exemptive authority could be used. Also, the industry was keen on it. It could be used for certain transactions that didn't merit legislation, and the Commission could have more authority in that area. People were nervous about giving the Commission that much authority because it enabled them to do something like Regulation ATS. But the Commission has so far exercised discretion in using that authority, and I'm sure if we don't we'll be talking to Congress about it.

But I don't know that Congress wants to get involved in the minutia of the markets unless they need to. Regulation ATS works now in our current framework. If we need a different framework going forward, we will have to go to Congress. Obviously, we can't continue to use the exemptive authority to change the entire '33, '34 and '40 acts and whatever other acts you might need changed. There will come a time when we need to go to Congress but, right now, as we continue to cobble together regulations to protect the investors and to promote fair and efficient markets, we are okay with the exemptive authority.

[83] Securities Act of 1933, Section 28, General Exemptive Authority. The Commission, by rule or regulation, may conditionally or unconditionally exempt any person, security, or transaction, or any class of persons, securities, or transactions, from any provision or provisions of this title or of any rule or regulation issued under this title, to the extent that such exemption is necessary or appropriate in the public interest, and is consistent with the protection of investors.

CHAPTER 7: DEVELOPMENT OF ALTERNATIVE MARKETS

Moderator – William Lupien
Matthew Andresen
Ian Domowitz
Kevin Foley
Raymond Killian
Arthur Pacheco
Gerald Putnam

Panel Discussion

LUPIEN: The development of alternative trading systems or markets is something that has been going on for roughly the last 30 years. This panel is unique in that each of the participants, at one time or another, came out of the trading business, including our lone academician, Ian Domowitz. I want to start with Matt Andresen from Island. It's been reported in the news that Island is intending to file as a stock exchange.[84] I understand the process can be daunting. I am curious to know if this is true and if so, why you would do that.

ANDRESEN: We believe competition is good, and I think everyone here agrees on the benefits of competition. Here's an illustrated example. I remember when I was a kid and they were going to deregulate the phone industry and break up Ma Bell. I remember my parents saying, "Oh, this is a terrible idea. Ma Bell works. Why would you want to break up something like that"?

I didn't think anything else about that until a couple of weeks ago when I was watching some movie on TV. I can't remember the plot, or if there was one, but I do remember a woman. She was in terrible danger and she had to alert her son to some kind of problem, so she picked up the phone, as everyone would do. The tension builds, there was the psycho music in the background, and she was listening to "beep, beep, beep, beep." It was a busy signal. She said, "I'll try again later."

[84] Island filed an application with the Securities and Exchange Commission to register as an exchange, on June 28, 1999.

How could she put up with that? I saw the size of the lapels and thought, this was a time that we didn't have deregulation. We didn't have competition. We didn't have the increase in service that I believe competition brings. It wasn't that the service of Ma Bell was bad, it was just that it could have been better. And better service is best achieved through competition. I believe competition always increases service and reduces price.

We've had tremendous competition, not only in our industry, but also in the brokerage industry as a whole. We've seen the enormous benefits of competition reveal themselves in the past five years. We've had competition within the markets. It might be time to have some competition between the markets.

Island is very excited about the opportunities that the Commission has put forth for us. We can continue to be an NASD registered broker/dealer and be subservient to them, or we can be an exchange ourselves and be regulated directly by the SEC.

The thing that we are bringing to the table is a competitive outlook. The competition that everyone here has brought to the Nasdaq market, could have equal benefit for a broader range of products, including the New York Stock Exchange. Allowing a direct, electronic mechanism to flourish is a tremendous competitive alternative. We are excited that the regulatory structure will allow investors to vote with their feet and go to places where they can get the best execution. The end beneficiary of any competitive environment is not my fellow colleagues, but the consumer. In this case, the consumer is the investing public.

LUPIEN: I suppose any of us could have filed as an exchange in the past if we wanted to, but we didn't. What has changed? Is it the result of the new regulations? Admittedly it's a long process. Is that part of the change, and what are the economics surrounding your decision?

ANDRESEN: What has changed? We now have the ability to choose whether to be an ATS or to go directly to the SEC. The most important thing, to us, is to be free to expand the breadth of product, perhaps to have representation in big board stocks, as well as to compete in the area of quote fees and market data. There has been a proliferation in the dissemination of information over the last few years. This is a more important subject and, within an acceptable regulatory framework, competition could bring down those costs.

LUPIEN: Let me throw this one out to the entire panel – are there any other panelists who are willing to state that they are going to file to be an exchange, or are the rest of you deciding to remain as broker/dealers?

FOLEY: On the matter of being an exchange versus a broker/dealer, there are four basic issues. First, there are access fees if you are an ATS or ECN.

Second, there's print revenue if you're an exchange. It is just a calculation as to which forum you get more revenue in. Third, there is the ability to trade listed stocks if you are an exchange. Right now the order handling rules have to be fully implemented for listed stocks. The adopting release on order handling rules in 1996 said the Commission would bear down if it didn't happen, and the adopting release in December of Reg. ATS said the Commission would bear down if it didn't happen. Commissioner Unger, this afternoon, said that they are going to bear down if it doesn't happen, but it hasn't happened. And Island's action reflects the frustration that you may have to be an exchange to belly up to the listed stocks.

The fourth issue is exchange regulation. The concept release of a couple of years back, which was not a proposal but a set of ideas put out for comment, said that we are going to have pilot programs for the exchanges. The release also tiered regulation for alternative trading systems that want to be regulated as exchanges. The tiered exchange stuff was all done a year later when Reg. ATS was proposed. It's not in Reg. ATS, and Commissioner Unger said that the Commission was going to take a look at that, but that is a significant obstacle to being an exchange. I think everyone here recognizes it. Some of us have to take more cautious stances with respect to our customers on issues like this, but those are the four factors that you have to weigh. Being an exchange is less attractive if the order handling rules are fully implemented for ECNs.

LUPIEN: So, are you going to file as an exchange?

FOLEY: No. We would consider it if it were advantageous for our customers. On April 21st, it will be advantageous for our customers, for us, to be a Reg. ATS broker/dealer.

LUPIEN: Does anybody else want to take a crack at it?

KILLIAN: We have no plans to file for exchange status. The activity in Posit, which is the system most people refer to, is analogous to that of a broker/dealer operating electronically. We do not post bids and offers and there is no price discovery in the system, and so far there doesn't seem to be any overwhelming demand to change the operation.

LUPIEN: Jerry Putnam, is Archipelago and/or Terra Nova going to become an exchange?

PUTNAM: The best answer I can give is I think so, probably, maybe, yes.[85]

[85] Archipelago filed with the SEC for exchange registration in August, 1999. Then in July 2000, Archipelago announced plans to join the Pacific Exchange to create a new market called the Archipelago Exchange, subject to the approval of the SEC.

LUPIEN: Artie Pacheco? I don't want to leave Strike out on this question.

PACHECO: In the face of so much regulatory and market structure activity it would be premature for us to commit one way or the other.

LUPIEN: Strike is somewhat unique among the new ATSs in that your investors are the bulge bracket brokerage firms in the industry, who pooled not only their financial capital, but their intellectual capital, which may be more important to developing an electronic system. Can you explain what was behind this collaborative approach?

PACHECO: We did it that way specifically because of Instinet. Start from the premise that my background is thirty five years of over-the-counter trading. In my previous position as a trading department manager, I saw profit margins continue to shrink and the cost of doing business continue to rise. One of those costs was the cost of brokerage or the cost of hiring an agent to represent my interest or to execute on my behalf.

There are two primary ways to execute an order. First, to book it yourself,[86] which is increasingly expensive in this volatile environment. Second, to find a natural other side, which is difficult for a broker/dealer who actually has less tools at his disposal today than he did just a few years ago. It's difficult for him to even speak to a competitor. Even if he is able to find a competitor who is the natural other side, there is no guarantee that that competitor will want to write the ticket with him at a favorable price and he is not likely to divulge his true level of interest to a competitor.

Instinet, the only neutral tool that we had for quite a few years, was effectively a monopoly. Monopoly is not a dirty word. A monopoly can be beneficial when it guarantees essential or critical goods or services in return for a fixed return, or no profit at all as a public service. The classic model is the public utility. The problem is that there is no room for competition and, therefore, no pressure on pricing and little incentive to innovate and change. Because Instinet had a monopoly, they were arrogant in their pricing and their technology. It became particularly onerous when Instinet decided to go into competition with its own customer base, which I also can't blame them for because they were capturing a significant market share and wanted to leverage it. We run a business like any other. It doesn't matter whether it's a candy store or a broker/dealer, you have a cost of doing business, and a cost of a product.

In this particular case, we had a research budget of over 100 million dollars. When an institution would call in the morning that was not a free order. In addition to the risk capital that you might be asked to put up to

[86] "to book it yourself", means to be the contra-side of a transaction on a principle basis. In other words to assume the full risk or to "bet" against your client's order.

work that order, you also had costs associated with being there to capture the order. The costs included your research analysts' salary, your salesman, your sales trader, the cost of turning on the lights and maintaining a market for the security so that you could be there to capture that order.

You take this commodity that cost you real dollars and has an implied value (because you are not collecting a commission on O.T.C. securities), and there is an opportunity to turn a profit. Failing to find the other side in the normal way, the only tool that we had available was Instinet, which meant essentially subsidizing a competitor. Because what we did was to hand it off to Instinet and they charged us for the privilege of shopping it back to our own customer base and selling it as liquidity that they were providing. But it is really our liquidity and our customer's liquidity. Then they would try to convince the customers that the next time there was no reason to bother with the intermediary, since they were the source of the liquidity. Great business for them. Terrible business for the broker/dealers.

We thought, given the state of technology and communication today, that we could build a better mousetrap. We could build it in a way that was cheaper to operate because our business model was different. At the same time, we would provide the same functionality that we could use for ourselves, because we use it to execute our customers' orders, and to liquefy proprietary positions. That is basically the genesis, and it's a consortium of firms in order to provide the "critical mass" necessary for a commercially viable trading system.

LUPIEN: Kind of sounds like the story told this morning, of everybody getting around the Buttonwood Tree in 1792. But in this case, everyone is getting around a computer system and creating a new exchange-like system, because it's not a sole proprietorship or a sole entity that is doing this, it's a group of you doing it. I am not saying that there is anything wrong with that. It sounds just like an exchange to me. And yet, right now, you are saying you probably wouldn't go the exchange route, or at least it is too early to know.

PACHECO: I'm saying that it's premature for us. There clearly are some benefits associated with being an exchange, but there are also some extraordinary burdens. We will leave the option open. I am not prepared to make that decision yet.

LUPIEN: It's interesting that the Commission came out with this new regulation and we, at this table, have a split opinion. In the past, I've seen something come out and most of the time everybody goes one way. At least we have one brave soul out here that is going to go for the exchange route.

Ian Domowitz, there are two areas that we often don't talk about in terms of automated trading systems. The first one that I'd like you to comment on is automation in the bond market.

DOMOWITZ: The bond market association's review of its own markets crossed my desk recently. It includes a special section on automated systems in bond markets and, traditionally, that section simply has something about inter-dealer trading.

Currently, there are six different initiatives plus one operational automated trade execution system for bonds covering a variety of aspects of the market. If you have a historical perspective on this, you realize that this was once the state of the equity markets. You could read reviews like that roughly one decade ago. Now we are looking at a variety of initiatives to bring automated trade execution into the bond market. There is going to be competition in that sector.[87]

Competition will be aided and abetted by another development that does have something to do with regulation. Recently, Chairman Levitt made a speech promoting transparency in the bond markets. The NASD, in its responsible fashion, put together a committee to study this. The committee's charge is to set out a framework within which prices will be reported more fully to the regulator and to the public.

One of the things that has assisted in the development of automated trade execution and alternative trading systems, not only in the United States in equities, but also abroad in derivatives, is more information about prices and volumes. This isn't a free-riding issue. People pay for this data. It allows the operation of trade execution services as a separate business. More fully reporting bond prices and volumes will encourage development in these markets. It won't take the bond markets ten years to catch up, because the technology is much better than it was a decade ago. The business models are also better developed now.

LUPIEN: Kevin, do you want to comment on the ATS and the bond market?

FOLEY: I agree with Ian Domowitz's point that there is a lot coming in the fixed income world. Chairman Levitt has basically fired the starting gun, and a lot of projects are off and running, to bring greater transparency, access, and ultimately liquidity through the same kinds of tools that equity traders have been using for years.

[87] More than 40 automation initiatives now exist, on a global basis. See, for example, "Stars Seen Aligning for Electronic Bond Trading," Bond Week, June 14, 1999.

LUPIEN: Ray Killian, would you comment about electronic trading in the options business? In particular, I wish we had somebody from the ISE[88] here because I would like to hear what they have to say.

KILLIAN: Actually, we don't have any plans on the drawing board, but I think that the development of ISE is very interesting. Our firm is involved in the crossing business, and is primarily known for Posit, the portfolio system for institutional trading. We are also a software company in brokers clothing. We have three hundred employees. One hundred and fifty of them are scientists and software developers. We build electronic trading systems. Quantex, the first trading system we built, actually has a foundation for trading electronically in the options area. It was built to analyse the relationships between cash and derivative markets. We adapted it to the equity market. We are looking forward with some interest to the ISE developments. It could lend itself to all kinds of immediate cash and derivatives strategies. I think it's long overdue.

LUPIEN: Ray, you have essentially been institutional only. Are you planning on entering the retail end of the business?

KILLIAN: No, not as the business is currently formatted. Our client base is entirely institutional. The size of retail order flow doesn't match up well with our particular kind of business at the moment. There are a couple of demographic reasons why retail doesn't fit us very well right now. Retail investors, as you heard a few times earlier today, are immediate gratification folks, and the passive core group of investors who are trading in Posit are just that, passive. The two don't match up very well. The payment for order flow is still an issue. You cannot agglomerate retail order flow and expect folks to send it into our system. I suspect Schwab will probably send it to Mayer & Schweitzer[89] before they send it to a Posit system for crossing at the mid-point, even though from a fiduciary sense it might be the right transaction for the retail client.

The other fundamental consideration is the contra-side credit issue. For me to set up an apparatus at ITG to monitor contra-side retail credit doesn't make much sense. If I knew that the collecting agent (that is, the broker/dealer on the other side) is the contra-side to that risk, I would be much more comfortable having him settle against the Fidelity transactions.

If at some point we can find a way to electronically sweep out the other systems into the Posit crosses six times a day as they occur, that would

[88] The International Securities Exchange (ISE) began trading on May 6, 2000.

[89] Mayer & Schweitzer, Inc., a subsidiary of the Charles Schwab Corporation, was renamed Schwab Capital Markets L.P. on March 1, 2000.

certainly add some liquidity to the system. Then we'd look at retail, but not as it's currently structured.

LUPIEN: Several of you operate these systems and, in fact, do talk to retail. Matt Andresen, would you give us some idea of the number of transactions a day, on average, that Island is doing?

ANDRESEN: First, a small clarification. Island is not an on-line broker or a brokerage house itself. We do not have retail customers or traditional customers that come directly to us. Everyone comes in through a sponsoring broker/dealer. We have about 200 broker/dealer subscribers, and that is the extent of our subscriber base.[90] With that said, we presumably did come from a primarily retail background.

We are now averaging about 300,000 executions a day, and in January 1999 counted for about 95 million shares a day in Nasdaq.[91] Volume is king. The way to quantify the value of a network, or an ECN, or an exchange, is to come down to volume, because that is the ability that you have to find a contra-side.

If you wanted to sell a car, you would never go to Amish country. You would go to northern New Jersey where you have to climb over the SUVs just to cross the street. It's simply a matter of going to the place where everybody else is. And as that place becomes larger and larger, it becomes what we call a virtuous circle, or snowball. Because it is big, it draws more volume. And hopefully, we reach that critical mass point on Nasdaq stocks. We would love to be able to translate that into a greater, better product, but there is no number I can put on a critical mass.

LUPIEN: It's about 300 to 400 shares per transaction?

ANDRESEN: The average execution size is approximately 300 shares. The average order size is approximately 600 shares.

UNIDENTIFIED MALE [From the Floor]: How much of that is internal matching and how much is coming through SelectNet?

ANDRESEN: That's an excellent question. Back in 1997, all of it was over SelectNet. But that number has decreased dramatically. Last August, our

[90] As of February 2001, Island has more than 500 subscribers, among them a growing number of institutional investors who access Island through an affiliate, Island Execution Services, LLC.

[91] During January 2001, Island executed a total of 7.86 billion shares through 26.9 million trades – a 43% increase over the previous months volume. In December 2000, Island executed approximately 1 out of every 7 trades in Nasdaq stocks (14.4% of all trades), according to data released by NASD's Market Data Division.

own matches were just under 50%. In January, that number was up to 73.8% of the matches that occurred.[92] This was Island subscriber to Island subscriber, not involving Nasdaq in any way. We think that number is a good quantification of the efficiency of our system versus Nasdaq. Obviously, due to the delays inherent in the Nasdaq system, the Nasdaq participants coming through SelectNet are adversely effected due to the time delay. So we expect that number to continue as Island has more subscribers and more orders.

Another metric you can look at is that, five quarters ago, for every four orders that were entered into Island, there was one execution.[93] Now it is around two to one. It's purely economics at work. If you put a couple of marbles in a box and shake it around, how often are the marbles going to hit; a couple of times? But if you put 500 marbles in a box, then shake it around, you really are going towards an efficient marketplace.

LUPIEN: Jerry Putnam, how many transactions on average size at Terra Nova?

PUTNAM: We are about the same average size, although we have a pretty good balance between retail and institutional customers. Our retail orders are about the same size as Island's. The institutional customer average order sizes are three times as large. But our retail orders are about the same size as Island's. We are doing between 60,000 and 70,000 executions a day. That is with both Archipelago (the ECN) and Terra Nova (the retail broker).[94]

LUPIEN: Kevin Foley?

FOLEY: We're averaging over 25 million shares a day, and somewhere between 18,000 to 20,000 executions. But we're in a different sort of business. We are an ECN, but we're in it for different kinds of customers. The service that our business provides is to the institutional-sized order. Big problems are faced by the institutional-sized order. And as of April 21st, if you are going to use a continuous price discovery visible system, it's got to be linked to the national market system. An institutional order has got to be displayed and interacted with the rest of the national market system. That is a

[92] In February 2001, approximately 94% of Island's executions were internally matched (subscriber-to-subscriber).

[93] In February 2001, approximately one out of every three orders placed on Island was executed.

[94] In January 1998, Archipelago became a broker/dealer and in April 1999, Archipelago and Terra Nova officially became separate entities. Gerald Putnam is CEO of Archipelago and sits on the board of Terra Nova. As of November 2000, Archipelago was doing an average of 164,000 trades and 80 to 90 million shares per day.

gigantic benefit to the institutional trader who, in the past, has gone to a pool of liquidity that is 10%, 15%, or 20% of the market. This is, 100% of the market liquidity is now available. If you use any one of our ECNs, you can trade with any of the other ECNs. Many of us are, in fact, connecting directly to each other in order to improve on the connectivity that Nasdaq provides, and to save some Nasdaq fees.

It's important to realize it is one world out there. We value volume and size for its perception value. It makes us look big, we get noticed more, and people say nice things about us. That helps us to make warm calls to our customers who have large orders to work. But, effectively, we could represent one customer in the new environment. Our mission is to use innovative tools to make it safe for the large order. We want to enable the million-share order to trade with the 300-share order and not push the market 15 points away. We attempt to do that by stepping invisibly into the crowd and taking the liquidity that is there, whether it's from market makers, order entry firms, options market makers, program traders, retail, or on-line.

LUPIEN: Artie Pacheco, how about Strike? I know you are new and you may not have numbers in the category that the previous gentlemen have been talking about, but where do you stand in volume and transactions today?

PACHECO: Kevin Foley is right. We serve different customer bases. Ours is very specific, brokers, dealers and financial institutions. We don't do any retail business directly and I would like to say we never will, except never is a very long time. I expect we never will. For credit issues mostly, but also because we feel that's the purview of our customer base and we don't want to cross that line.

We have been operating for about a month and a half now, with only five of the partners participating. It's a limited rollout until we are comfortable with the technology. Then we will continue doubling and tripling the number of users over the next couple of weeks.

At this time, we are averaging a million and a half shares a day, and our average trade size is about 1,600 shares. The average order is somewhere between 5,000 and 10,000 shares. Because there are only five participants so far, the contra-side, for the most part, is SelectNet accessing our book. That brings the execution size down.

ANDRESEN: I would have to say that Kevin Foley is right, also. Every one of us has slightly different business models, all trying to serve a different base, or to serve it in a different way. This leads me to another plug for competition.

When the SEC enabled us to have representation on the box, there was really just one player out there. Now you have all these different players all doing slightly different things. There are new strategies like OptiMark's,

Tradebook's, and Strike's, all trying different solutions. That is the beauty of competition. It's up to the investors to decide which ones suit them best. And I think there is certainly room for different solutions to all these problems, and this demonstrates that if you open the doors to competition, people will step in and fill the vacuum with new and different ideas.

CORMACK: Matt Andresen, I have a question for you. About eight months ago, I saw that you were offering a two-tier rate structure. That is, if you posted a bid or offer on Island, you would get a lower commission rate versus hitting a bid or taking an offer. This is a kind of liquidity fee. Have you been able to figure out a way to pass that on to the end customer, not just to the broker/dealers? Was it a successful strategy to build order flow in your system?

ANDRESEN: That is an excellent question. First of all, I hate to call it a two-tiered system because everyone pays the same thing.[95] But you are right. Each side of the trade pays something different. If you think of Island as being a big grocery store, what we are trying to do to build volume on our book, is to have stuff on our shelves. I grew up in North Carolina. Every time there were snow flurries, people didn't just buy out all the batteries. They hoarded Twinkies and lettuce and everything else.

It's kind of like what we are dealing with in this market. People are hungry for the product, and the product, in this case, is orders, it's volume. What we are trying to do is get people to put orders on the book, to add liquidity. Now everyone pays the same price, whether you come off the street, whether you are a subscriber, or whether you are a non-subscriber coming over SelectNet. You are paying the same one-quarter of one penny per share.

But, if you are one of the people that put the order on the book, and it is subsequently executed, we will pay you a tenth of a penny a share. So we have an average of 20 or 30 subscribers who actually get checks from us at the end of the month for providing liquidity. We take the difference of .0015 cent per share. We have been doing this since June and certainly we've added great volume.

In terms of passing it on to the end users, it's not possible for us to do that, and for a very good reason. The end user, coming through a subscriber, trades with complete anonymity. We know only the broker/dealer. That is very important to us for credit issues and also for the anonymity of each individual broker/dealer. So, it's not possible to know who the customer is and it's not possible for me to pass it along. But the real value to the customer is the

[95] Currently, institutions, select subscribers, and non-subscribers had a separate fee schedule.

liquidity. If he does 100 shares to the extent that he wants his dime, he will have to talk to his broker about that.

The real advantage to the consumer is the ability to gain representation in the market, which is what people have been able to get with all of our systems, and to get it fast, efficiently, and have the ability to get a very quick execution that might happen due to liquidity.

LUPIEN: I thought it would be interesting to hear each of your thoughts on where this is going to be five or ten years from now? Let's start off with Jerry Putnam.

PUTNAM: In the U.S., we're going to go to shareholder-owned, non-member, for-profit exchanges and, most likely, public companies. This is not ten years from now, but a lot sooner than that.[96]

FOLEY: I can't look that far in the future. But I can say that on the 12, 24, or 36 months horizon there will be trends toward both diversification and consolidation. I don't believe there will be a trend toward fragmentation, because the result of the order handling rules will be a consolidation and nationalization of access to liquidity. Competitors are going to gain and hold their positions in the marketplace by being innovative, and by providing better service.

You'll see some convergence between continuous markets and call markets, and fancy tools that bring together large orders, such as OptiMark. It's all going to be made possible because access to liquidity is available to everybody. The innovations that gain you market share in the year 2000 will not protect your market share in 2001. All of us are going to have to be constantly innovative, constantly on top of our game, and constantly providing good service. But the good news is that there is every indication of a willingness in the institutional customer community (and the brokerage community as well) to pay for value, and that will continue to be there. That is why people will continue to innovate and compete.

KILLIAN: Well, I agree with a lot of what has been said. One of the most exciting developments I predict is the electronification of the markets in Europe. When you compare the size of the North American market with the European market, you see an EEU that is 20% bigger, and rapid growth in the direction of automatic access. If I look at it from our company perspective, I get excited about the potential.

[96] On January 4, 2000, the NASD board approved a major restructuring and recapitalization of the Nasdaq stock market. In the new ownership structure, NASD will own only 22% of the Nasdaq stock market and the remaining 78% will be owned by investors who will consist of current NASD members, issuers and strategic market participants. http://www.mfcafe.com/pantry/ls_wb_011700.html, January 10, 2000.

Also, an explosion in technology. The consolidation that Kevin Foley and Jerry Putnam referred to is going to drive people toward another rapid expansion in the use of technology.

DOMOWITZ: One of the first things that is going to happen is that the question Bill Lupien first asked Matt Andresen, whether he would register as an exchange, will become a moot point. We will learn to separate the regulation of financial market structure from other areas of concern, both here and abroad. That question literally will not be asked any more.

There will be a merging of companies around this table, maybe not with each other, maybe with other people. There is certainly going to be a consolidation in that sense. However, that is not a consolidation into one single large pool of liquidity. I see many pools of liquidity separated by different characteristics, as has been mentioned at this table. We're going to have a branding of trade execution service companies. The brands will go beyond the NYSE and Nasdaq. It's possible that Island will become a brand. It will be associated with a certain liquidity pool that it has developed. It may ally with other companies to achieve that. I think we will come to the realization that echoes Mr. Syron's remarks earlier today. We are looking at a bunch of firms here. I think this panel really brought that home. It's not traditional national exchanges anymore. This is a business where different trade execution services are offered, embodying different technologies, and choice of trade execution also means a technology choice. There are also communication technologies. A lot flows from that in terms of predictions for the next ten years.

I'll give you a wild one. There are going to be worldwide, organized cartels of trade execution service providers. Not only that, the regulators won't need to worry. It will be socially optimal to formulate because it's going to stimulate R&D and, indeed, trading services provision. That's my crystal ball.

PACHECO: Probably the most exciting thing that is going to happen in the near future is the globalization of markets. Trade barriers will go down because they must. Advances in technology and communication are going to make it easier for you to have instantaneous access, on a cost efficient basis, across national boundaries and currencies. The abilities of U.S. investors and foreign investors to cross-invest will explode, to the benefit of everybody.

We are beginning to recognize that different investors have different needs. There will be different mechanisms that evolve to serve the specific needs of certain investors. We also have to recognize that different types of issuers have to trade in different environments, or we risk the possibility of a serious dichotomy in the way equities are traded. However, ultimately, that would be beneficial because it implies a recognition that they should trade differently.

I am concerned with the shift in investment philosophy in this country from investing to short term trading (essentially gambling), and what that might mean for the capital formation system going forward. It is unclear how far this trend will go or what the long-term effect will be on capital markets.

But the positives lie in the coming together of communication and technology, and the world of possibilities created by this union. These will enable us to operate more efficiently and to provide more products and services to our customers. The biggest wild card is the empowerment of the consumer by technology and how we will need to respond to his or her demands.

ANDRESEN: The only prediction is that things will be better and things will be cheaper. Let me continue my phone analogy, where 20 years ago we had busy signals. In my building there used to be a little cubby hole where this guy had a coffeepot, and he sold coffee for 50 cents a cup. I don't know if he went out of business because of Starbucks, but he is gone. There was an empty space there for a while, but now a cellular phone store moved into the tiny space. You can't walk into the building without guys saying, "Here's a fully digital, hand-held phone for free. Free minutes, please take it." Is it a good business for them? Who is to say? But it's better for me because I am a consumer of telecommunications services.

I think we're going to have, just like we have in telecommunications or any of these deregulated industries, an increase in service and a reduction in price. It's not for us to say who will win. That's for the investors to decide. But there is probably room for many people.

LUPIEN: We will now open it up for questions from the floor.

TIMOTHY BAIKIE [From the Floor]: I found this panel very interesting because we are anticipating that our security administrators are shortly going to be issuing a proposal for ATS regulation in Canada.[97]

I have two questions for Matt Andresen. One, if you become an exchange, do you see yourself performing a listing function? Secondly, what SRO obligations are you going to have on top of what you're doing now, and how are you going to discharge them?

[97] In July 1999, the Canadian Securities Administration (the provincial securities regulators acting jointly) issued a proposed regime that would allow Alternative Trading Systems to operate in Canada. It would have allowed ATS operators to register as broker dealers without being required to register as stock exchanges. The proposal attracted considerable comment and was reissued for comment in July, 2000. Although numerous changes were made, ATS operators would still have the option of registering as dealers. Final rules are anticipated to be adopted in early to mid-2001.

ANDRESEN: In terms of the listing function, I think that listing a stock is a form of bonding for the individual company making the list on the New York Stock Exchange and meeting their high standards. It is a form of credit or bonding on the quality of the company. Listing, however, does not have to be tied to the particular meeting place where a trade occurs. I do not think that, in the immediate short term, we will be doing that. Certainly, I'm not going to rule it out for sometime in the future. But it is not crucial to our business model at this point.

As for your question about the SRO function, Island is a highly technical organization. We consider ourselves experts at it, and to that extent we take a lot of pride in innovating. However, being an exchange obviously implies a steep increase in other responsibilities. We are going to take them very seriously. We have already hired a general counsel who has experience, not only with the SEC, but with building exchanges as well. He was previously working with the formation of the over-the-counter markets in Eastern Europe, specifically, Romania. The SRO obligation is going to create a lot of challenges for us. That is the part of our infrastructure that we have to beef up the most. In making our exchange filing, the regulatory aspects, both through stock watch and audit functions, are big issues that we are going to have to tackle head on.

HANS STOLL [From the Floor]: I was struck by something that Kevin Foley said about ECNs connecting directly to each other to avoid Nasdaq's fees. It sounds like a second market of markets. Do we have an infinite regress here?

FOLEY: We don't spend a lot of time thinking about a lot of highfalutin concepts. We look at it as missing messages and paying a dollar a message for that fact. We are obligated by virtue of the ECN rules to be connected to each other through SelectNet. But some of us got together and said, "There is a better way."

If the Next Nasdaq proposal that was withdrawn, or if another form of that proposal is submitted, there is underneath that proposal through the SOES mechanism, we think, an attempt to make all messaging and all trading go through the Nasdaq central computer. Then Nasdaq creates, through its regulatory position, Nasdaq as its own monopoly technology provider. But we think that private firms using state-of-the-art connectivity, which we don't have through Nasdaq, could do a better job. That could be strangled by regulation, but it does represent improved service for our customers and reduced costs for us.

UNIDENTIFIED FEMALE [From the Floor]: Which ECNs are connected with which others?

ANDRESEN: First of all, everyone is connected to everyone else through SelectNet. We could also have the same subscriber relationship with another ECN that we have with our other subscribers, so we have subscribers that are ECNs. But, honestly, we can't say who they are.

FOLEY: It is a technology issue. Every ECN has traded with every ECN today. We are all connected already. If we find better and cheaper ways to do that, away from Nasdaq, that may have implications that are beyond a businessman's ability to consider. We are just trying to do a better job for our customers and we are all already connected. Every ECN trades with every other one today.

PUTNAM: When you think about it, the SelectNet connection is faster, it's cheaper, and you have taken a third possible failure, the Nasdaq potential to fail in-between, out of the equation. It's not political.[98]

FOLEY: Market makers can also connect to us by private connections instead of coming through Nasdaq. But market makers can't do that to each other, and we can't do that going out to market makers, because of SOES. They don't want to fill an order coming in and find out that they got hit on the head with a Nasdaq hammer right afterwards. So the drive to extend SOES to ECNs and to solve the SelectNet problem by saying, "We won't hit you over the head with two hammers any more, we are just going to hit you over the head, Mr. Market Maker, with one," leaves the market makers thinking, "Oh my, that isn't a very big improvement."

Nevertheless, at the end of the day, if Nasdaq gets their way, Nasdaq will be the monopoly technology regulator, and we ECN's won't be connected to each other anymore. We will all be trading with each other through Nasdaq. We'll be trading with our own customers through Nasdaq because it will be a safer way for us to execute internal orders; namely, to go out to Nasdaq and come back. That's a serious concern.

ANDRESEN: It's a case of, "The chain is as strong as its weakest link." Everyone else will have to "dumb down" their systems and get their speeds down to the lowest common denominator. I think that's anti-competitive.

ALLAN GRODY [From the Floor]: A quick question. Market orders versus limit orders: which of you don't take one or the other or both and in your statistics, how much is market orders and how much is limit orders and what are the implications depending upon the size in terms of pricing off of other markets?

LUPIEN: That is an important question. But I'm not sure we have time to

[98] Direct connections between ECNs and market makers has continued to grow and has allowed continuous trading through these connections when the SelectNet system has been down.

go through all of the panelists, so I will ask them to answer that privately.[99]

Let me close by making my own prediction. Volume will exceed anything we can imagine in the next ten-year time frame for a variety of reasons, many of which we can't even conceive of today. My second prediction is that the regulatory arm of the SRO will be spun off. This is my own personal feeling. I think it has to come. I do not like the idea that a regulator can come in and through the regulatory arm force people to do something that isn't the correct thing to do. I doubt very much that I have any argument from this panel.

Thank you.

[99] The question was intended to understand if and how ECNs and ATSs were exercising their fiduciary responsibility to provide market orders (non priced orders) with the best available price at time of receipt of order. Generally only priced limit orders drive electronic limit order books. Market orders typically represent about half of the orders received under the traditional market maker structure of the Nasdaq. Most electronic limit order books do not allow market orders. Instead they ask the order placer to substitute a priced limit order within the National Best Bid and Offer to represent a market order (referred to as a marketable limit order).

CHAPTER 8: IMPLICATIONS FOR INNOVATION, COMPETITION & EFFICIENCY

Moderator – Daniel Weaver
Douglas Atkin
Frank Baxter
Peter Madoff
Jeanne Murtaugh
Evan Schulman
John Woodman

Introductory Statement

WEAVER: A couple of months ago, Bob Schwartz and I were talking about what we could do to make this conference special. Bob said, "Wouldn't it be great if the Dow hit 10,000 the day of the conference"? As you know, Bob knows a lot of people, so he called up Governor Pataki, and as we speak there is a heavy buy program being launched by the New York State Pension Program to push the Dow over 10,000. So in the future, whenever you hear about the Dow at 10,000, you will think of the Zicklin School of Business at Baruch College. It was the "Zicklin rally".[100]

The order handing rules and technology have caused a wave of new entrants, as we heard in the previous panel. We have also seen a consolidation of existing structures, both domestically and internationally. These consolidations have taken the form of outright acquisitions (Nasdaq and Amex), or cooperation agreements (e.g., the Canadian exchanges, Copenhagen-Stockholm).

We have had a lot of dramatic changes. The ATS rules due to be effective next month, will bring further change to the industry by allowing some of the new entries to become exchanges. This will enable new exchange rules to be tested without prior SEC approval, and will bring about greater pre-trade transparency.

[100] Unfortunately, that day the Dow reached a high of 9960.71 and closed at 9879.41.

Also looming on the horizon are penny ticks.[101] Academics agree that if smaller ticks cause smaller spreads, many investors are going to switch from limit orders to market orders.

We also agree that the providers of liquidity will be reluctant to reveal their orders as soon as the price of stepping ahead of those orders becomes negligible under penny ticks. Will investors withhold liquidity and increase the volatility of markets? Or will technology simply allow liquidity providers to hold on to their orders? In essence, this could create a fragmented limit order book that supplies liquidity to the markets just in time to prevent volatile swings.

There is increased pressure at home and abroad to increase pre-trade transparency. Exchanges around the world have adopted the SEC mantra that transparency is good. The SEC often states that sunshine is the best disinfectant. As a gardener, I know that not all flowers flourish well in full sunshine. In particular, the market quality flower will wilt under full pre-trade sunshine. I guarantee it.

I have just finished the first draft of a paper with Ananth Madhavan and Dave Porter, where we examine what happened in the Toronto stock exchange when they opened their limit order book to the public. Spreads widened and price volatility went up. Also arguing against pre-trade transparency is the fact that, under the old Nasdaq system, if market makers wanted to narrow the spread and lay off a position, they had to identify themselves. That allowed for retaliation against the spread breakers and the continuation of this collusive behaviour.

Then the ECNs were brought in. Since the ECNs have been made part of the NBBO, all a market maker has to do is send an order in through an ECN. They receive the anonymity the ECN provides, and they can narrow the spread without the fear of retaliation. So the ECNs have actually made our markets, in some sense, more opaque. And this has done what? It has narrowed the spread.

In light of these ongoing changes, the goal of this panel is to offer perspective on how we got to this point and on how the pre-existing structures have responded to this dramatic change and increasingly dynamic trading environment. We are not just talking about government regulation here. We are not just talking about the SEC. The SROs have also sponsored measures that create competition with current members.

[101] A pilot group consisting of 13 listed stocks and related options began trading in decimals on August 28, 2000, at a penny (.01) MPV. Seven of the issues were New York Stock Exchange stocks and six of the issues were American Stock Exchange stocks. On January 29, 2001 all remaining NYSE stocks were converted to decimals.

For example, Nasdaq has an agreement with OptiMark that, in some people's eyes, creates direct competition with Nasdaq members who do institutional business. Nasdaq has also discussed a CLOB that many members condemn as additional direct competition to traditional Nasdaq business. How did the old guard, if I may use that term, respond to these government and SRO regulations?

Our panel brings a unique perspective. Doug Atkin is CEO of Instinet. Instinet's customers can access 40 securities markets throughout the world, so Mr. Atkin can give an international as well as a domestic perspective to this discussion.

Frank Baxter, the CEO of Jefferies, has been an active participant in our markets for quite some time. He can bring a view from the trenches of how we got to where we are. Peter Madoff's firm has been very vocal with NASD's members concerning the SRO's proposed rules. John Woodman of UBS Warburg brings the European perspective to our panel. Perhaps John can answer why we don't see ECNs being created in Europe – or will we? Evan Schulman of State Street and Jeanne Murtaugh of BNY ESI, round out our panel; they will tell us how institutions are responding, or will respond, to the various regulation induced changes.

Panel Discussion

WEAVER: Let's start with Frank Baxter. Frank, you have been around a while. We have heard the academic perspective on how we got to where we are today. What is the view from the trenches? How did we get here?

BAXTER: Well, I would say strategy is made in the trenches, Dan. I think that Dan's comment about the market going to 10,000 was the first time today that we have talked about the underlying thing that we are trading. And in Wall Street this morning, Jim Glassman, who is a great libertarian thinker, proposed that the Dow was going to 36,000. That puts all the discussions we have been having about the arcania of trading into perspective.

The reality is, there is value behind the companies that is reflected in the little pieces of paper that we exchange back and forth. As we get all bogged down in our business and regulation, we begin to feel that we are the saviors of the market. Well, the real savior of the world is the American economy. We play an important, but minor, role in that effort.

We have talked a lot today about the regulation of 1975. At that time, a great innovator, Don Weeden, was changing the way share ownership was exchanged. In 1974-75, about 19%, 17%, something like that, of all volume was done in the third market. The exchange, realizing that fixed commissions were going, cut a really good deal with regulators and Congress, saying “we’ll give up fixed commissions if you will give us barriers to entry,” so that no one could get in for the next 20 years. The regionals at the last minute got the ITS in there so they could get in on the deal. Any system can be gamed. Bernie Madoff very innovatively said, "With ITS, we can get the middle as a broker/dealer and beat the exchanges."

Some competing systems were able to penetrate the barriers to entry set up for the exchanges. Posit came along. Instinet had a grandfather clause and Bill Lupien, as a trader, saw a replacement for the $2 broker. The $2 broker used to be a guy with a big liver who would get between the buyer and the seller.

What we had from 1975 until recently was stasis, which is one function of regulation, to keep things as they are. But now, all hell has broken lose. We have the order handling rules and despite what Erik Sirri said about volatility, the Securities Industry Association has published a paper that says that volatility has increased significantly in 1997 and 1998.[102]

I know other things have happened besides the order handling rules. We've had the Asian crisis and other sources of volatility, but it probably is no coincidence that volatility has increased. A metaphor for pre-order handling rules is, stores on a block called dealers, who said they would always buy or sell shares at a price. With the order handling rules, the cop who usually polices that block said, "It's all right to set up a little stand right in front of that store now and to come and go as you like." The almost certain result is that those stores will close down. This may or may not be a bad thing and we may have evolved to that point anyway. But it looks as though we're going to an end of the affirmative obligation of market makers. Stabilization of the market will come from other sources, probably the corporations themselves, who are much more active, and from institutions.

Based on history, three suggestions to regulators are: (1) try to have humility, (2) try to do no harm, and (3) try to abstain. We have a tremendous economy and tremendous market makers. I'm not all that concerned about the day traders. I know it's a unique phenomenon, but I remember in 1987 some very respectable people putting full-page ads in the Wall Street Journal saying, "Program trading is going to kill us." Then the market learned that these dumb programs coming in were a great opportunity to take advantage of.

[102] Schaefer, Jeffrey M., “Explaining Recent Increases in Stock Market Volatility,” Securities Industry Trends, XXV.1 (January 29, 1999); 1-11.

I love the regulators. They teach me tolerance, patience, a little good will, and they are part of the American tradition. But they should endeavor to get out of the way of innovation. In 1850, there were 250 exchanges in the United States. Just like in the money management business, you have the consolidation at one level and then proliferation of great new specialized services at another level. Historically, that is the relation between regulation and innovation.

WEAVER: Thank you, Frank. Evan Schulman, you have a unique spin on this. Could you tell us what it is?

SCHULMAN: Commissioner Unger and Frank Baxter have both given us a description of what has happened. Let me just rephrase it, but with a spin.

The exchange act controlled exchanges very well until the mid-60s. It was a nice, stable platform. Somewhere in the mid-60s, institutional demands for liquidity became irresistible. Something had to break. So we started to innovate. You found things like the upstairs market, the first infant steps of electronic trading occurred, and we were off and running. The end of that first phase was, of course, the introduction of negotiated commissions. All that did was to increase the volume. So there was still more need for more innovation, and it continued.

Bob Schwartz, in moderating the first panel, referred to this as an "earthquake." That is very hard to control if you're a regulator. The ATS system and regulation have now thrown open the regulatory net. If you talk to knowledgeable people, they say the ATS regulations are incredibly ambiguous and they cover virtually all of us.

My Machiavellian training would say that what is going to happen in the future, once the regulators see the structure of trading in the future and it's fairly obvious what is going on, is that they will tighten up again. Then we will return to a controlled, stable platform. The implication for the businessman is, if you are going to do something, do it now. Perhaps when financial history is rewritten, they will say that this was our finest hour.

WEAVER: Evan, on another note, you are Canadian by birth. In early March, the Canadians announced that they are going to consolidate their trading on different exchanges. What do you think the chance of that happening in the U.S. might be? There are some people who think we should do that in the U.S. Or do you think that people are just predicting the end of the world? They did that when we relaxed branch banking and people thought we were going to go to twelve banks in the U.S.

SCHULMAN: I went to the University of Chicago, and I have a deathly fear of monopolies. They stifle competition. My advice to Canada is, "don't do it." If they do, the liquidity will move down here.

WEAVER: But it has moved down here. They have consolidated to compete with us.

SCHULMAN: Yes, okay, but size is not everything, as the growth of the ECNs is demonstrating.

WEAVER: Frank Baxter, do you see a role for a central exchange in the future? How many exchanges should we have, and in what kind of form?

BAXTER: There is definitely a role for a central marketplace. I would guess that's been the history of consolidation. We use the word competition a lot. It is a word that regulators, who aren't generally in competition, like to use a great deal. What we heard in the last panel was much more about niche building. In nature, competition involves people finding a place they can defend. But we romanticize competition and make it like a sport, where you kill each other at the end of the hour. That really isn't what competition is about. It would be well worthwhile to remember that the real function of competition isn't just knocking each other's heads off all the time. That is wasteful.

WEAVER: John Woodman, what can we learn from the European exchange affiliation trend, and why don't we see ECNs in Europe?

WOODMAN: I will start by picking up on some of the European experience and the effects of competition between exchanges. The early '90s saw some very inefficient markets in continental Europe. The London Stock Exchange's SEAQ International, captured a lot of market share from those European markets.

So, the first lesson is, if there is natural liquidity and international investors are seeking to trade European securities, then market structures, in one way or another, will adapt to meet that natural liquidity. That is the point Ian Domowitz was making about what happened in the 1960s. That is what is actually happening in Canada right now. It's not so much the formation of a monopoly, it's the ability to have effective competitors that matters. Who knows what the end result will be?

Europe showed that a particular reaction to market structure can rarely be defined because, if you have an open competitor situation, other things will change. What happened was that the European markets reacted. They took a major leap forward, and almost all of them developed electronic central limit order books. These books were very successful in trapping the liquidity back into their own individual markets.

That is probably the main reason why I don't see ECNs as they exist in the U.S., developing in Europe. Because, effectively, they're forming the function of bringing together the limit order prices. If the electronic markets already provide limit order books, there isn't a value added for an ECN.

However, I can see that the ECN technology may well provide order routing mechanisms from end investors directly into the exchange.

Consider the consolidation in Europe, the proposed alliance that was announced between London and Frankfurt recently, and some of the Scandinavian alliances. You could call these monopolistic, or you could call them a reaction to future competition. The exchanges in Europe are right to be concerned. Who knows what's out there? There are a whole lot of new technology providers. And there is a feeling that they have to get their act together as a single currency, and effectively have one common economy in Europe. It's going to take some time. There are an awful lot of structural barriers. There are still different tax schemes, different saving schemes, different languages, and different cultures. There is an awful long way to go before there's a single European market, but it's coming.

I think the exchanges are all a little scared of being a niche regional exchange that will be put out of business, as all niche regional exchanges have been in the past. They have reacted in the most sensible way, which is to be part of the end game by being a catalyst of what happens in the future and of developing scale.

I would be very surprised though, if the end game were one European alliance or one major stock exchange. Simply because if there is, and we experience a growth in natural liquidity, that market structure will not suit everybody's needs. Then lots of competitors will come up and do something different. I suspect what will also happen is that regulation, or the demand from the end investors, will force some sort of National Market System. Whether it's a series of different entities, or one, you could say it doesn't really matter.

WEAVER: The fact that you have CLOBs in Europe is why we don't see ECNs?

WOODMAN: Exactly. Yes, that is right.

WEAVER: So then all we have to do to solve all of Nasdaq's problems is to create a central limit order book and make everything price and time priority. What do you think about that, Peter Madoff?

MADOFF: Going back a bit, firms like ours are products of technology and deregulation. The desire is to use those two very important factors to find a niche, and possibly to provide liquidity. That is one reason why you don't have the ECNs and/or the same scenarios in Europe. We've been over there for many years, and our experience is that there were not a lot of firms that wanted to provide that liquidity.

It's a given that if you are going to compete for order flow, you're going to take market orders along with limit orders. When you take limit orders, you are forced to provide print protection and limit order executions to your clients who are competitively expecting liquidity. One of the things that ECNs do, for those people who don't want to take the responsibility of taking the limit orders directly into their quote (which again gets back to the order handling rules), is that the ECNs provide them with order books.

To my knowledge, a lot of the reason why the CLOB was there in Europe, was that firms were not looking to provide liquidity or to take the responsibility of holding or protecting the depths of their books. In the U.S., many market makers, like myself, were opposed to Nasdaq's and other's initiatives for CLOBs because they were not giving us the chance to compete for limit orders in a fair and equitable way. I don't think that the CLOB itself is the issue. The issue is having the advantage of technology. Its all about networks and connectivity. Nasdaq is in an incredibly good position to provide total openness to their network, for all of its members who choose to compete for order flow, whether it be through limit order protection, market order liquidity, narrower quote increments, instant liquidity, or a whole assortment of competitive tools.

The long and the short of it is, competition is about being able to do something that the other person isn't willing to do. Competition is a good thing. I don't think everybody should have to compete all the time, but the facilities of a CLOB in many ways don't allow people to compete, because they become de facto safe harbors. That was the biggest fear the market making community had about limit order books. We were concerned that our ability to say, "we're going to give the print protection, we're going to do all the necessary things," was not embodied in the proposal. The openness to fair and equitable competition through the network was not there. That's not to say we couldn't have possibly had something.

I think many of the market makers were looking for a compromise that the SIA put forward, which was very fair and equitable, but didn't come about.[103] But I don't think people are against limit order rules. The order handling rulings are appropriate. I think the new ATS release is a remarkable document for what it says, and what it doesn't say. The key embodiment is competition.

WEAVER: Doug Atkin, what do you think?

ATKIN: I agree with John Woodman. You cannot look at what is going on in the United States without seeing it in the global context. I agree totally with John's account of what took place in Europe. The European exchanges

[103] For further details, see the SIA Comment Letter dated May 4, 1998 Re: Securities Exchange Act Release No. 34-39718; File No. NASD-98-17, www.sec.gov/rules/sros/nd9817n2/madoff1.htm.

only chose to innovate when they were faced with the choice of innovate or die. Could you imagine having 50% of our national market trading in Canada or Mexico? That is exactly what happened in Holland, in Switzerland, in Italy, etc.

It was only in smoky rooms in various continental European countries, when the head of the exchange called the boys in and said, "Look, we got two choices, to die or to innovate." The Europeans innovated.

In our opinion, that is the model of market structure, and whether we know it or not, there is serious gravitation pulling us towards that structure. In every major European market right now, you have a voluntary central limit order book. You do not have to use it. The exchanges are viewing themselves as businesses, and they're building systems that people want to use. Therefore, eighty percent of the liquidity matches in Europe are not through regulatory fiat, but through the development of a business model. You have the ability to trade upstairs and there are no display issues. If you build an efficient central market, people will choose to go to it. You actually have, believe it or not, electronic futures markets standing side-by-side with electronic equity markets, and you have electronic settlement systems linked up to each of these. That, in our opinion, is the model of market structure and, whether we know it or not, there is serious gravitation pulling us toward that structure.

Compare that to what is going on in both exchanges here in the United States. The current situation, particularly in Nasdaq, is unsupportable. You have – and I tend to be fairly animated about these topics – an absolute Frankenstein. It's a merging of orders and quotes somewhere between the old market and some new market. I venture that we shouldn't be arrogant enough as Americans to say there isn't a better model out there. I am not anti-American at all. I'm just saying we've seen this movie play before, six hours ahead of us and, rather than play around with multiple ECNs – in an efficient market, there is no such thing as an ECN.

Let me say one more thing regarding the SEC. We agree one hundred percent with the Commission's objectives. I give them a lot of credit for being out in front and saying America needs a new market structure to take us into the new millennium. The current market structure has shown serious wear and tear, and I would argue that it's cracking. It's up to those people in the industry, who all share a collective interest, to not move incrementally. When the jet aircraft came into existence, the propeller maker's response was a turbo prop. But the turbo prop lasted for a short, short period of time.

An ECN is a turbo prop. It's up to the industry to move responsively. At Instinet, on a daily basis, we do 150 million shares, single counted. We trade everyday in Nasdaq stocks, and we feel strongly that it's our responsibility to migrate that liquidity into a new market structure. We are not protectionist about where it goes. We would like people to join us in getting Nasdaq to a new place.

CORMACK: I have a question for Doug Atkin. We talked about the evolutionary aspects of where we need to go. Is that possible under the current government structure of the NYSE and Nasdaq?

ATKIN: You've hit the nail on the head, Mike. This is a political problem, not an economic problem. Peter Madoff said he would not be against a central limit order book as long as it was voluntary. We think it should be voluntary, too. But there are a lot of people who do not want that to happen. We could make it happen in two weeks, but it is a governance issue. You buy the technology from one of the European exchanges, you put it in place, and you keep your block desk trading upstairs. It would save the big wire houses significant amounts of money in their block trading, because you would still have your upstairs block trading in the listed market for those who wanted capital. Capital plays an essential role in any market structure, even though Instinet chooses not to provide it. It is critically important for investors who want to have it.

Now, the fall of communism took a lot longer than people thought, but you turned on CNN one day, and it had happened. I predict that's exactly what is going to happen in this industry. And the people who are moving incrementally will be left behind.

BOB WOOD [From the Floor]: If Nasdaq develops a central limit order book, does that compete with Instinet?

ATKIN: We think that would be for the good of the market. Instinet got a bit complacent with its position in the industry. We acted like we had a big business to protect and weren't interested in taking market structure forward in Nasdaq. That would be a partially valid criticism of our firm. But those days are gone. We want to move Nasdaq forward.

We feel, as Bill Lupien said at the end of his session, that any time you give the market a more efficient structure, volume explodes. It's good for all participants. If Nasdaq builds a central limit order book that is voluntary and that treats all members on an equal basis, we are for it.

MURTAUGH: Doug, this is interesting because ultimately what I hear you saying is that you do not view yourself as an ECN. Do you consider yourself as an agent to the process?

ATKIN: I don't care what we are called. We are in the business of getting orders executed and providing best execution to clients around the world in major markets. Our business model outside the United States has nothing to do with Instinet providing a central limit order book for those markets. Europe is the fastest growing piece of our business. And the European markets are the most efficient markets in the world. We have a model that uses technology and neutrality and provides investors unique access to pools of liquidity, as well as the ability to trade blocks upstairs. That is where we think Nasdaq should go.

MURTAUGH: The reason I asked that question is because we are an agent. I don't know how well people here know ESI, but ESI was born of regulation in 1976. The little known Instinet of that time, we were the first broker/dealer to take electronic orders institutionally. And we are exclusively institutional. We were founded by Morgan Stanley as a response to the deregulation of commission rates. It was recognized that reduced commissions would require electronic order handling and routing for trades of a certain size, in order to be profitable. We grew to have the facility to operate internationally, and by the late 1980s we were in the trade order management business. We were one of the first brokers to interconnect and integrate, from the portfolio and trader management systems to markets in and beyond New York.

We built connectivity to Peter Madoff. We had the ability to go to Instinet. We could go to ITG if our clients wanted to. However, in 1988, most of the clients, and we are speaking purely institutional, stated that they were not interested in anything but New York. Three or four years ago, when approached by Bloomberg, we created Tradebook, a sister company that is the facilities manager to Bloomberg's ECN. So, as an organization, we are a pure agent.

We have not participated as visibly in the market place as the other panelists here have done. We were born of change, and have continued to change, based on our understanding of regulation, and on our understanding that it is technology that drives regulation. If you consolidate a lot of the discussions that were held today, you could conclude that there will be pools of liquidity. Trade execution services, and how you serve the client through connectivity, is ultimately going to drive the efficiencies of the market.

What I have heard today is basically from the standpoint of institutions. They face more challenges than they faced two years ago. You have to deal with solutions that can be achieved. You have to define the solution that works best for particular market segments. The reason why Instinet is where it is at, more than anything else, is because it had a great business model. If you cannot define a good model, you are not going to be in business, just as Doug Atkin has stated.

So the reality is, you use a business model that is driven by cost, is driven by control, is driven by connectivity, and ultimately is driven by choice. The challenge I would put to the audience, particularly those in the institutional business, is to really know exactly what it is you want, because when we're looking to build it, or to move towards solutions, there has to be a clear definition of what the consumer wants.

WEAVER: Some here forecast the death of ECNs within two years. Does anybody want to respond to that?

JAY PEAKE: Both ends of the table seem to be saying that the solution to this is price and time priorities, a limit order book, and electronic execution. If that is true, what kind of a percentage cost savings is that to the investors totally? Today's investors have to pay for every system we have, and all the inter-connectivity. Ian Domowitz and I came to the same conclusion. It would be about 10% of the cost. One order of magnitude less if you had a fully electronic, price time priority order book system. The customers would benefit from the 90%.

ATKIN: We would agree with that. We do a lot of transaction cost analysis and we've been active in the European markets for quite awhile. In the European markets, on the top 40 stocks, where there is deep liquidity in their index stocks, the costs are lower than trading in Nasdaq, and give New York a run for their money. I would say it is better for investors to have a deep pool of liquidity.

One point on fragmentation. At the end of the day, competition is excellent because it forces people to innovate. Both the buy-side and the sell-side want one deep pool of liquidity per instrument. In the foreign currency market, which is something our parent company had a substantial share in for many years, a consortium formed to give Reuters a go for the foreign currency business. What has happened is that EBS,[104] which is a competitor of Reuters, controls 95% of certain currency pairs, and Reuters' currency trading system controls 95% of other currency pairs.

I think the current situation in the equity markets is bizarre. What you're going to end up with is competing exchanges. But, just like in the listed market, one exchange is the primary exchange. The issue is, what is that deep pool of liquidity going to look like? It's easy to decide how it is going to be structured. The models are in Europe. But what is the ownership structure going to be? That is the big political problem.

WOODMAN: However, you could argue that a number of the European exchanges have adapted without changing their political structure. The political structure came afterwards. It's a political process.

[104] EBS is an electronic broking system for interbank foreign exchange. It is a Partnership comprising the subsidiaries of 13 major market-making banks and the Minex Corporation.

We haven't compiled the same level of empirical evidence about cost reduction. My answer would have been "quite a lot," in terms of reduction. But I think what you say about the spreads in the major European stocks, compared with some of the spreads in the U.S., sounds intuitively right.

The U.S. market appears to be a successful, liquid market, simply because there is so much natural liquidity. Two things are competing on this side of the Atlantic: deficient market structure and natural liquidity. I suspect that Europe is coping with a lack of liquidity, but has a pretty efficient market structure. An awful lot of demographic trends in Europe and economic restructuring are going to take place that I hope will increase the natural liquidity.

WEAVER: What is this liquidity? Is it dealers providing liquidity, or is it customer orders providing liquidity?

WOODMAN: It's customer orders, ultimately. That is my meaning of natural liquidity. Ultimately somebody on the other side wants to buy something or sell something.

WEAVER: Peter Madoff?

MADOFF: Let me clarify something. I am not in favor of the consolidated limit order book. I think that, in lieu of market makers, dealers, and ECNs or any registered broker/dealers who choose to compete either as agent or as principal, where there is no other mechanism to provide those services, then and only then, should the network spring in. But until such time as you have the network connectivity and those people who choose to compete and provide services, those services should be free and open to all the members who are going to responsibly compete for that order flow. Only when there is nobody there, do the limit orders become the issue.

The key point for me is what Doug Atkin said. There are only 40 European stocks that have liquidity all the time. There are many times you're not going to have that continuous flow of liquidity. Then dealers, market makers, upstairs traders, and everybody else, must be there to bring the markets into some degree of equilibrium, albeit temporary.

That does not necessarily mean it's the best of both worlds. It is a reality that has been working very well in this country. You should not take away the incentives for broker/dealers to act as either principal or agent, and to respond to, and interconnect and interface with, the market structure. The network has to be open to its members. The SROs should not be building something that competes with its members. Only where it is not available, then and only then, should that mechanism come about.

WEAVER: What about Nasdaq entering into an agreement with OptiMark?

MADOFF: I have no problem with Nasdaq entering into an agreement with OptiMark, so long as anybody else who wants to be in that environment can come, interconnect, and be doing it. The issue for Nasdaq and OptiMark was the fact that it seemed to be a unique agreement, not something that was open to all. There was also some question as to how much Nasdaq was providing funding with its members' money. This might be at odds with its own memberships' specific desires to compete.

I am not an expert on OptiMark. I am sure everybody has got his or her own opinion on it. I think the real issues are openness, connectivity, fairness and choice.

WEAVER: Doug, what do you think about the OptiMark agreement?

ATKIN: I have a lot of respect for what Bill Lupien has put together. OptiMark does move market structure forward, and anything that moves market structure forward is positive for investors. I wish Bill all the success in the world, and think he has got a good start. The relationship between OptiMark and Nasdaq is complex, and it probably could have been handled in a better way. But, all in all, we're in favor of it.

JIM ANGEL: I want to echo what Peter Madoff said about incentives. In all this discussion of a centralized limit order book, we have to pay careful attention to the incentives for market participants to provide liquidity. Many people make the false assumption that a limit order book means that one must have time priority as a secondary priority rule. Most markets do not use time priority as their only secondary priority rule. Most markets have an extraordinarily rich and complex set of incentives designed to create liquidity.

As we discuss innovation and market structure, and the regulation thereof, we need to keep those incentives carefully in mind. Otherwise, simply going to a CLOB with time priority because it looks clean, may end up throwing out the baby with the bath water. So, if we want people to provide liquidity, we must give them incentives to do so.

BOB SCHWARTZ: I have a question about the CLOBs in the electronic market of Europe. The order flow in the U.S., for the most part, is much more institutionalized. You don't just put institutional-size orders on a limit order book. We would need more structure for that. When people talk about one size not fitting all, it isn't just cutting across shares and different stocks, it's also cutting across different orders. Even for the biggest stocks, a couple of hundred thousand share orders require special handling. We can't just put them on electronic limit order books.

SCHULMAN: If I may comment here. When you put a limit-order on the book, you are giving the other side an option to pick you off. You can value that option. If that order is out of your control for five minutes, then using

Black Scholes, the value is two to five cents a share, depending on the volatility of the stock and assuming $40 stock.

ATKIN: If that's the only way. I agree with Bob Schwartz.

SCHULMAN: The thing is, you should be very careful about your transparency rules because you could destroy your markets. We are back to the incentives that Jim Angel is talking about.

ATKIN: Agreed. What our clients are telling us through their analysis of transaction costs is that, if you have an efficient central limit order book, it should handle between 60 and 80% of the volume in any given instrument. If you want special handling for your large orders, the brokers should bash each other over the head to compete to provide the value added above and beyond the capabilities of the central limit order book.

But it's in all of our best interests to have a central facility that provides a good price benchmark. It is, of course, possible to move half a million shares of BMW or any major European stock by putting it out into the central limit order book, but don't do it in one piece. Or, if you want capital throughout the day, pick up the phone and call the big firms to move a block.

SCHULMAN: Another way you can do it is to allow for hidden orders. But those orders have to go to the back of the queue. The hidden orders can't take priority over the orders that show. Market orders then get price improvement from the hidden orders. The New York Stock Exchange has done great things advertising their price improvement.

WEAVER: Let me follow-up on that. Toronto has done away with their hidden limit order feature. Doug, you said you supported the SEC in their goals. But you didn't support the SEC when they wanted you to do away with the reserve function for institutional orders at the inside quotes, and asked you to reveal them all.

ATKIN: Yes, absolutely. We were not supportive of that. We believe that what the Nasdaq market needs is a strong, deep, but voluntary and efficient limit order book that operates based on strict price/time priority and is open to all Nasdaq members. Members could redistribute that technology to the institutions and, yes, institutions should have direct access, too.

Even with a voluntary and efficient limit order book, we think that the upstairs market will continue to be necessary for achieving best execution or orders that require special handling – such as institutional block orders. Whether this upstairs activity takes place through an electronic screen or over the telephone, we believe that there should be one transparency standard for upstairs trading across the market. Any regulation mandating pre-trade transparency requirement for upstairs trading should apply not only to electronic agency brokers, but also to upstairs dealing firms. That is the disagreement we had with the Commission.

WEAVER: It's important in any central limit order facility to have the ability to attract market orders that come in. I don't think Nasdaq's previous proposed limit order system, Next Nasdaq, ever really did that. Could I ask the panel to make a final comment if they wish?

WOODMAN: For a period of time in Europe in the early to mid-'90s, you had a central limit order book operating in competition with a dealer capital market. The dealer capital market died because the institutions preferred to have the combination of trading in the way Doug Atkin describes – essentially a voluntary central limit order book, complemented by trader capital, and complemented by brokers providing order management services. There is a lesson from Europe there.

SCHULMAN: I would reiterate that we are now in a period of change; Regulation is as loose as it is going to get. Enjoy it, it isn't going to last very long. If you're an ECN, make your money now.

MURTAUGH: Technology will provide solutions that are not obvious today. Whether we have a central limit order book or adopt some other form, there is ultimately an opportunity for those organizations that understand service and good business models.

MADOFF: The discussions about a central limit order book may all become moot next year when we go to decimals with no minimum increment. Think about that.

WEAVER: The end of Nasdaq as we know it.

BAXTER: In thousands of garages across America, people are thinking of ways to trade things better. We had better watch out for what is coming. I think a uniquely American central limit order book will evolve, kicking and screaming, without being dominated from above. And there will be new ways to split up risk, if we can ever connect the futures market with the cash market. We're in a very, very exciting period, and we ain't seen nothing yet.

ATKIN: I would agree with all the comments that my colleagues made. I think this is a period of serious transition, and it calls for non-incremental behaviour to go to the next market structure. As much as the brokers and the ECNs compete with each other, there is a bigger interest that is creating a far more efficient way to trade OTC stocks. This will benefit investors and intermediaries, and will lead to an explosion in volume.

WEAVER: To paraphrase Franklin Roosevelt, the only thing we have to fear is change itself. Thank you very much.

CHAPTER 9: THE REGULATORS' PERSPECTIVE

Moderator – Maureen O'Hara
Alden Adkins
Brandon Becker
Robert Colby
Edward Kwalwasser
Ruben Lee
Ernest Patrikis

Introductory Statement

O'HARA: A longstanding theme in economic research has been, "does regulation lead markets or follow"? We don't necessarily know the answer but, if we rephrase it, "do regulators lead markets or follow," then, given the order of today's panels, we know the answer. We are last.

We have heard a lot about regulation today, some of it complimentary. But most of it suggesting that the nice thing about being a regulator is that there is always something to do, or not do, as the case may be. When you think about the evolution of villains over time, you can go back to the evil landlord, you can go back to the tight-fisted banker, you can go back to the Wall Street tycoons. But in today's setting, it is the attorneys in Washington who have become the new villains.

Our regulators face a daunting task as they try to sort out what has become a difficult problem. Indeed, if you were to draw one key conclusion from what we have been hearing today, it is that there are doubts that the current regulatory structure is working, or that it is well suited to the task.

I suspect even members of this panel who are involved in this process have doubts, if not about their own regulation, certainly about the regulation that others are doing. Each of the panels today has focused attention on this issue. We learned in the panel this morning, that we might be ruining the price discovery process by allowing so many providers of services. This and other issues being addressed today are not trivial questions about how to tinker with the system.

We've heard that the cross subsidy approach used to pay for regulation doesn't seem to fit in a modern market. The SRO approach may not make sense any longer. There are political as well as economic problems. The issues that have been raised in this conference are fundamental, including the very interesting problem of the role of information.

As our trading systems evolve, the following is becoming clear. A large part of what we are seeing is the evolution of trading platforms that provide information. Who owns that information? How is that information distributed? What are the transparency rules? That is the name of the game for regulators.

Panel Discussion

O'HARA: Let me start with a question for Ed Kwalwasser. Are we over-regulating? For example, does the extension of suitability standards to Internet trading indicate the strength or weakness of current regulations?

KWALWASSER: The real question is not whether you're over regulating or whether you have good or bad regulations, but whether you have appropriate regulations for the market. Ours is a market where individuals meet institutions. We believe that is part of the reason that people come to our market rather than all of the ECNs we see out there. There are markets around the world that would love to trade the stocks that we trade, but people come to our market because they feel that they are being treated fairly.

In about 1985, the SEC proposed a rule dealing with insider trading. Foreign countries and everybody said the SEC was being overly aggressive. The Commission was being a colonial power trying to export its insider trading rules to the rest of the world that had none. Then what happened? Margaret Thatcher decided to privatize in England, and when she did she realized they needed some individual investors. They couldn't privatize and sell it all to the few pension funds that are managing money in the U.K. All of a sudden, they had insider trading restrictions and other rules to encourage the individual investor to come to the market. And all across Europe, the same thing happened.

I was speaking in Germany a week before they instituted their insider trading prohibitions a couple of years ago. The head of one of their markets was complaining that they couldn't raise money for small and medium-sized companies in Germany. So I threw out my speech and got up and told them, "Of course you can't. Without rules that would encourage the individual investor to enter the market, Germany is not going to be able to sell stock in small and medium-sized companies. You have to look at the market and at the kind of investors you want to attract, and then determine whether the regulation is appropriate."

UNIDENTIFIED MALE [From the Floor]: Let me add a slightly different perspective. I think there is a serious question as to whether the institutional side of the market is over-regulated. In fact, we have a release out now inviting comment on getting rid of or creating new exceptions for institutional customers. Ed Kwalwasser is absolutely right. On the retail end we need to be sure we are protecting people and encouraging them to enter the market. But there may be room for more deregulation on the institutional end.

O'HARA: Ernest Patrikis, do you have a comment on that?

PATRIKIS: Well, I happened to come across Arthur Levitt's February 24th testimony before the Senate Banking Committee; "All investors deserve the same protection regardless of where they choose to purchase their securities." Then he goes on to say, "and especially recommending only suitable investments." I looked at the suitability rule when it came up in the context of the U.S. Government securities. An institutional investor dealing with a dealer is protected by a suitability requirement. While there is a safe harbor out of the requirement, the dealer cannot be absolutely sure it is in the harbor.

And that goes for SROs. They are not SROs, they are DROs. They're "delegated regulatory authorities." When an SRO acts, it is the United States Government under the jurisdiction granted it from Congress through the SEC to the SRO. But why does every rule change on an exchange have to be approved by the SEC?

I come from a banking supervisory background. The New York Clearing House operates the CHIPS[105] system. They system handles a mere 1.4 trillion dollars a day. When it changes a rule, it does not have to publish the proposed rule in the Federal Register. If the Clearing House wants to change the price, it does not need to publish in the Federal Register. The SROs are micro managed.

O'HARA: Bob Colby, as one of the micro managers, do you have a response to this?

COLBY: Well, I would bet you that The New York Clearing House doesn't make a single change without first checking with the New York Federal Reserve Bank. So, it's not a totally open and transparent process. The New York Reserve Bank, a semi-regulator, semi-government agency, pre-reviews whatever the New York Clearing House does. It's not as if they are free to go off and do what they want. The New York Federal Reserve people watch these clearing systems like a hawk, and they'll tell them if they think they are doing something that is inappropriate. We will never know what the

[105] The Clearing House Interbanks Payment System (CHIPS), was launched in 1970 by the New York Clearing House Association as an electronic funds transfer system. Currently it operates as a real-time, online payments system that transfers funds and settles transactions in U.S. Dollars.

Fed tells them because it's done in private over tea and cookies. But I would bet you that the New York Clearing House does not do things that the Washington Fed or the New York Fed hints are inappropriate.

We are talking about a transparent versus a non-transparent system, not about whether we are able to operate free of regulation and oversight. The banking system is subject to extreme oversight. But I think I got distracted from the main question.

O'HARA: Do you have a view on whether the wholesale markets are being over-regulated with suitability issues.

COLBY: Tell me who the wholesale markets are and I can respond better. But the SEC approved the NASD's suitability interpretation that basically said that you could look at who the investor is, and at whether they can make a reasonable judgement, and then change the suitability requirement.

Ernie Patrikis quoted from a speech that actually wasn't about whether institutions should be regulated. It was about whether bank securities activity should be subject to the same sort of standards. Arthur Levitt's point was that such activity should be subject to similar regulation.

PATRIKIS: The rationale in the banking world is the "no suitability" requirement. Instead, it's an "appropriateness" requirement. The worst thing an institution can lose is its reputation. Ask Bankers Trust. An institution, in order to protect itself from lawsuits and to maintain its reputation, ought to be taking certain steps regarding its customers. That is common sense. You don't need a suitability requirement to enforce it; you just need what is appropriate.

I know someone who taught new math. Some people came to evaluate her, and told her that she had to change the way she taught. The reason was she didn't teach the course the same way as everyone else, and thus they couldn't evaluate her. That is what the SEC is saying. You must do it the same way so you all can be regulated the same way. But this country is big enough, and its markets are large enough, to cope with some firms regulated as banks, some as insurance companies, some as security firms, and some people need not be regulated at all. Let the customer choose which he wants to do business with.

COLBY: The only difference I can see between appropriateness[106] and suitability[107] is who can enforce it. I read the appropriateness standard

[106] Appropriateness refers to the risk tolerance of an investor undertaking a particular investment and that investor's awareness of all procedures and strategies being employed to carry out such investment.

[107] Suitability refers to a broker-dealer's obligation to recommend only those investments that are suitable for a customer. To trigger the suitability obligation, a broker-dealer must make an investment recommendation to his or her customer

expressed in a number of contexts, and they all came down to a similar proposition. The only difference was that the investor couldn't enforce it. It's up to the bank supervisor to enforce appropriateness.

BECKER: I want to take this in a slightly different direction, and make a couple of quick observations about the question of regulation.

First, we have markets that are the envy of the world. On an empirical basis, no one wants capital markets like Europe. So I don't particularly want to hear examples of how it's done in European capital markets, because that is not a model for raising money, as Ed Kwalwasser just demonstrated.

Second, we have markets that have a lot of both individual and institutional participation, which is very valuable as a general matter. We are evaluating this in the context of an historical bull market. I would just raise a cautionary footnote that if we read this transcript three years from now, and the markets were to decline, this conversation will read very differently. If we see a dramatic decline in the market and a lot of carnage, even the appropriateness and suitability conversation will look very different three years from now.

Third, we now have individuals investing in the market in a way that is going to clamor for additional regulation on a continuing basis. If you paid any attention to some of the concerns about the role of monitory policy, you know that the ups and downs of the stock market are now the concern of central bankers in the context of interest rates. That is going to have an implication for oversight of security markets that goes beyond this.

My final point is that part of the debate should look to who is being regulated. Ernie Patrikis and Bob Colby were talking about institutions versus individuals. There are alternative market participants who look to try and provide competitive opportunities, and much of our model is built on either Nasdaq or the New York Stock Exchange. But we don't have a particularly good methodology for figuring out how to deal with new entrants and how to set standards that don't disadvantage those new entrants. This is an historic problem with regulation.

O'HARA: Ruben Lee, do you have any thoughts on the SEC's ATS approach and whether this is likely to work?

LEE: I have some comments on the ATS regulation. But I also want to comment on the issue of whether Americans are over-regulated. The market is in a jubilant state at the moment, in terms of innovation and the ability to raise capital, all of which are significantly in advance of Europe. Moreover, the real issue is, could we be better off with a different regulatory structure here in the U.S.? Forget Europe. I am more interested in market structure questions, than in suitability and appropriateness, regulation of fraud, or regulation of insider trading. Market structure questions concern the dissemination of information, order routing and order execution.

In my opinion, in many circumstances markets are better than regulators at determining optimal answers. Having just spent five months in a former Soviet Union country in charge of a project on the development of capital markets, I can say without question that the merits of mandated transparency can be high. Very high. However, here in this much more competitive environment, let me attempt to undermine a religious tenet. In my view, mandated transparency is not always optimal. Since the '75 Act, it's been part of the law, and the SEC is not at liberty to question the law. So, you can't blame them for following that rule. I use the example of transparency because it's one market structure issue for which there is still a wide consensus here in America. Namely, that mandated transparency is good.

However, I would argue that in many circumstances, private incentives will lead to the optimal provision of transparency. This is not withstanding the case of the Soviet Union where it must be mandated because there is so much corruption without it. I think that Reuters or Bloomberg could provide systems which are better and less problematic in terms of governance, and which would better enhance market performance, than the national market systems the SEC has mandated into existence.

Now, let me make some specific criticisms of the SEC's new ATS and exchange rule. I see three paradoxes or contradictions that are inherent in it, which I think will lead to problems. The first paradox arises from the fact that the SEC has historically said, and continues to say, that market structure should be determined by market participants, while at the same time it makes statements that misallocation of capital, wide-spread inefficiency, and trading fragmentation will occur if markets are not coordinated. So, on the one hand, market participants should determine market structure. But, on the other hand, we must have some form of coordination. So which should it be? We can't have both.

The second paradox arises from the very reason the new rule was proposed, namely that the distinction between what is an exchange and what is a broker has become blurred. I focused attention on this problem in my examination of the existence of the MONSTERs (Market-Oriented New Systems for Terrifying Exchanges and Regulators).[108] The paradox is that, despite the SEC's goal of clarifying which institutions should be classified as

[108] See Ruben Lee, "What is an Exchange? The Automation, Management and Regulation of Financial Markets," Oxford University Press (1998).

brokers and which as exchanges, the Commission has merely succeeded in this new rule in making the distinction even more opaque by introducing the new regulatory category of an "alternative trading system."

The final paradox concerns the possibility that regulation can help foster innovation, one of the SEC's key goals in introducing its new rule. As noted by Commissioner Grundfest, however, such a possibility is "a little bit of an oxymoron right there."[109] Just when the SEC should be encouraging new practices by exchanges in the face of an exciting wave of technological advances, one key effect of the new rule will be precisely the opposite.

In particular, in my view the optimal governance structures of exchanges as providers of markets is best left to the market itself. This is not to dispute the SEC's just concern that when exchanges operate as SROs, all the regulatory apparatus of fair representation and due process should be followed. But rather to say that this apparatus may well not lead to the best decisions being taken by the exchanges as commercial entities, and that the SEC should therefore allow the governance structure of an exchange's commercial arm to have a different form from that of its regulatory arm. In effect, the SEC already sanctions such a policy for alternative trading systems, by allowing them to operate under the regulatory umbrella of an SRO. The distinction between the commercial and the regulatory activities of an exchange, however, has not yet been recognized by the SEC.

SCHWARTZ: I would like to get to a another issue that is also integral to these regulatory themes. Much of what we have been talking about is governmental, the SEC and behind the SEC, Congress. But the other aspect that I find interesting is the SRO obligation. With the SRO responsibility, the regulatory function is performed by the entity that is also producing marketability services as a business enterprise, and it gets complicated. I would like to ask Alden Adkins from the NASDR and Ed Kwalwasser from the NYSE what their thoughts are about this.

ADKINS: Ed and I represent two slightly different models of answers to that question. And there is a third answer lurking out there, that I think we are moving toward.

Our model says that, within a larger corporate structure, you separate regulation formally. This is to nullify the conflicts, or at least the perception of conflicts, between the market and the regulation of the market. I think that works very well as a model. I don't think a complete separation is necessary to deal with the conflict of interest. Because of the perceived conflicts, the

[109] Hearing before the SEC (5/1/1989: 83).

SEC is absolutely right in allowing people to become an exchange if they want to get out from under NASD or New York Stock Exchange regulation.

The New York model, which we were using preceding our own reform, says "put it all in one place." That works fine. For a lot of different reasons, it may work better in an auction market than in a dealer market.

But in the end, because of the increase in competing exchanges and ATSs, we will move toward a single SRO. For economic reasons, as well as for policy reasons, we will move to the third model, a single self-regulator.

I disagree with Ernie Patrikis. Self-regulation is an appropriate approach, generally speaking. When you eliminate self-regulation, you end up with direct government regulation, which is not great. A completely separate, stand-alone market and member SRO is where we're moving, and that is the right place to be.

O'HARA: Ed, what is your view?

KWALWASSER: It's a little bizarre to think that the NASD is fooling people by having two corporate structures under one single board. It controls all of the rules, filing, and anything else that you do. It really comes down to whether you as a market, determine to regulate your members. A lot of European markets have given up being the regulator of their members, as opposed to being the regulator of their market because they were afraid to regulate their members. They were afraid to bring proceedings against them, so they gave it up in order to be a market. Our members understand that when they come in to be a part of the New York Stock Exchange, they can expect to be regulated as if we never saw them as a market participant.

We in the regulatory group, to the chagrin of people in marketing, don't share data. We protect data as confidential information. We have brought proceedings against our biggest members. We have brought proceedings against our smallest members. We have brought proceedings against people who have been on our board of directors. And we have brought proceedings against the children of people who have been on our board of directors. It really is determined by how you start out. If you determine that you're going to be a self-regulator and do the job, then you are going to do the job.

If you are not connected to a market, you might as well have government regulations. The whole idea was that the market was going to regulate itself, not that the members were going to regulate themselves. I don't think that we should move to a separate self-regulatory organization that is not attached to anyone.

It is nice to have the SEC overseeing us for three reasons. One, the government feels more comfortable. Two, it's a lot cheaper for the government to have an oversight role as opposed to a direct role. And three, I agree with Ernie Patrikis, a lot of our rules do not have to be vetted as long and as hard as they are, but I could understand why the SEC might think differently.

O'HARA: Suppose the NYSE goes through with their suggestion that they might buy an ECN, which would be set up as a proprietary firm that would generate funds for your members. Would it still be so easy, as you seem to imply, for an SRO to handle the function?

KWALWASSER: First of all, since we are a membership corporation, it's illegal for us to give any money to our members. So they won't get any direct benefit. Today, all of our large member firms trade something called 19c.3 securities.[110] They're just like an ECN. They trade the same securities that we are trading. In all of the years that I've been at either the SEC or at the NYSE, I haven't heard anyone come forward and say we are not regulating him or her appropriately because they are competing with us.

LEE: I substantially disagree with your statement. I don't know the law on the possibility of handing back money from, for example, an ECN run under a subsidiary. But I do know that in almost all exchange contexts there is a huge variety of ways to effectively hand back money. Lower cross-subsidies could be charged, and all sorts of different ways. Let me come to what I think is the crux of this issue that Alden brought up. The first question is, "what is the optimal governance structure for the trading system"? The second question is, "what is the relationship between an SRO and that government structure"?

The traditional governance structure has been one of a mutual exchange. There are good economic reasons for that. The prime one is that most exchanges essentially operate in a monopolistic manner. Take the NYSE, for example. It had a huge amount of the trading, so it effectively operated in a monopolistic manner. It is not a pejorative use of the word. The NYSE was the sole provider of trading systems for a wide range of securities. As a sole provider, it had the ability to do what all monopolistic providers do, which is to raise prices. If the users of the system are also its owner, the users can say, "we are going to determine that you don't set high prices for the users." That's a good economic reason for having a mutual structure when you have a fairly monopolistic environment.

What has happened now is that we have a much more competitive environment, in which the costs of mutual governance structure have become more apparent. One such cost is that of governing in a democracy where you

[110] In July 1980 the SEC instituted Rule 19c.3 on an experimental basis, freeing Exchange members to take off-board markets for issues that were listed on the Exchange after April 26, 1979.

have free-riding coalitions, it takes a lot of time and money to build consensus, and it is sometimes difficult to reach decisions.

In a more competitive environment, a for-profit corporate structure may be more efficient than a mutual structure. However, things will change very quickly, and we will probably once again get trading systems that capture a large majority of the trading. Then the attributes of the for-profit corporate structure, which look advantageous now, will quickly become less advantageous.

KWALWASSER: You are right Ruben, and that is why Congress and the SEC prevailed on the NYSE to have a public board. That is a very substantial brake on any monopolistic tendencies we might have. We have institutions on our board, we have public companies, and we have people from all sides of the industry who would not necessarily have consistent aims.

O'HARA: Let's open it up for questions.

DIANA HENRIQUES [From the Floor]: Mr. Lee, I was intrigued by your notion that mandated transparency might be necessary in the wild and woolly former Soviet Union, but that in the pure-hearted, clean-living, and completely law-abiding United States, mandated transparency would not be necessary because no one would do anything wrong behind closed doors. I've been covering financial fraud for about eighteen years, and that does not match with my experience.

You also said that you thought demutualized, for-profit stock exchanges would face clearer, cleaner lives than private companies in general. Again, I've seen private for-profit companies go somewhat astray from the straight and narrow. I am wondering where, in this new world, someone is going to be willing to pay for the kind of regulation that might still be necessary, given the laws of human nature.

Are you saying that we can afford not to mandate transparency in the U.S., because we are so much more honest, but that it is necessary over there to prevent corruption?

LEE: Absolutely! (Laughter). But that wasn't my point. My point was as follows. It is not the case that there would be no transparency without mandated transparency. Private incentives will lead to optimal levels of transparency. There is a big debate as to whether you need mandated transparency to stop fraud, which the SEC has argued. I have pointed out the merits of mandated transparency in the old Soviet Union. What I also said was that there are costs of transparency.

The SEC has painted a rosy picture, saying that transparency benefits all their criteria. I am less positive about that. Transparency does not always increase liquidity. And a lack of liquidity will allow for the possibility of greater fraud. In terms of the cleanliness of the profit-oriented corporate structure versus the dirt of the mutual club, once again that was not what I was saying. What I said was, you choose a government structure in order to minimize transaction costs. I gave an example of how a mutual government structure can help minimize the transaction costs that can arise if you have a monopolistic trading system. Namely, a mutual governance structure allows the users as owners to stop the organization from charging a high fee.

I then said that in a more competitive environment, it might be that a for-profit corporate structure allows you to get away from the costs of the mutual structure, where the benefits are not so great.

HENRIQUES: You are misunderstanding my question. In the private corporate structure, where are the incentives to regulate? It's a cost. It would be a disadvantage to the shareholders to do so.

LEE: I completely accept that, and didn't respond to that before. I think we will have to be more transparent about the cost of regulation. Maybe we should have a more explicit tax and perhaps stop the requirement for cross subsidies.

BECKER: As a former bureaucrat, I think that what you get under Ruben Lee's model is more transparency and less regulation.

O'HARA: Jim, do you have a question?

ANGEL: I'm kind of surprised that at this conference on regulation, no one has talked about the imminent demise of Glass Steagall[111] and the structure of regulation in the United States. We've traditionally had institutional-based regulation. We've got a regulator for banks, one for insurance companies, and one for securities firms. Actually several, when you consider futures and securities and so forth.

However, when you think about it, a lot of these financial service firms are basically doing the same thing. They are pooling small amounts of capital for larger uses. They are providing risk management tools. They are providing investment opportunities, and they are also part of the payment system.

It seems to me that a better way of regulating would be one in which we stopped looking at this institutional bias. We should step back and take a functional perspective. I would like to hear the regulators on the panel comment on what you think the regulatory system in the United States is going to look like in the next millennium.

PATRIKIS: If one business has an inherent disadvantage, let it disappear. This is functional regulation. Do you know what functional regulation means

[111] On November 12, 1999, the President of the United States signed into Public Law, the Financial Services Act of 1999. This Act amends the Banking Act of 1933 (Glass-Steagall Act) by repealing prohibitions against commercial banks (Federal Reserve member banks) engaging in securities activities and against investment banks engaging in commercial banking services.

in the United States? If a bank does it, some other regulator ought to regulate it. I haven't heard any coherent thought on how to do functional regulation.

Let's take a swap. A bank can do a swap. A securities firm can do a swap. An unsupervised, cross stream affiliate of a broker/dealer can do a swap. Or, an unsupervised, unregulated, swap dealer can have the hardest regulator in the world, the free market. And everything doesn't have to be treated the same. There is nothing wrong with the separate treatments. Why does everything have to be regulated the same? Who says that's superior? Let the customer choose what the customer wants.

Banks do not engage in volatile securities transactions, banks aren't dealers, but banks do have a lot of capital. There are different regimes for banks and broker/dealers. The regulators and supervisors don't even talk the same language. A bank supervisor remedies, a securities regulator punishes. While that is a black and white statement, it contains more than a kernel of truth. But everything doesn't have to be regulated. That's the first principle.

ADKINS: I don't know that I completely disagree with that, assuming you are largely addressing the wholesale market. There is a case that has been made for functional and equivalent regulation of people who are affecting transactions for, or advising retail customers on, securities transactions. I think people who are touching real world customers, not institutions, ought to be functionally regulated the same way and pursuant to the same structure. Actually, the biggest issue isn't so much the banks – it's the investment advisors who are in a completely different regulatory world, but who to a large extent are functionally doing the same thing. They are certainly making recommendations to real world people about securities transactions. This is a functional regulation case, at least at the retail level.

BECKER: My first prediction is that large institutions will be subject to some oversight due to concerns about systemic risk. Not withstanding everything else that people say, the LTCMs[112] of the world and the threat of the failure of major institutions will bring significant financial regulation to bear. I think there is a market for regulation, and one of the markets for regulation is the failure of large institutions. We will continue to see the consolidation of institutions, in Europe, Japan and the United States, and that will create demand for more oversight.

Secondly, we will continue to see, through privatization efforts, increasing individual investor participation in the markets. As a result of that we will see

[112] Long-Term Capital Management, a hedge fund in Greenwich, Connecticut, nearly collapsed after incurring large losses resulting from its investment activities. Ultimately, The Federal Reserve Bank of New York orchestrated a $3.6 billion bailout with 14 major financial institutions on September 23, 1998.

increased demand for something in the nature of fair treatment, whether we want to believe that regulators can do that for individuals in those markets, because people will lose retirement funds, people will see IPOs at exorbitant prices, and Internet systems will fail. That will generate a public demand for regulation. Because there are over 50 million individual investors,[113] that demand will be met. So, the two demands for the growth of regulation in the next millennium will be large institutions that are of global significance, and widespread individual participation through retirement pensions, advisory services and routine savings.

PATRIKIS: The systemic risk is over-rated. It's a term that is over used.

There are cases where a system can pose inherent systemic risk. But just because something is big, doesn't mean there is systemic risk. Some use mischaracterized systemic risk as a rationale for regulation. We have a good experiment with the FSA[114] in terms of complex financial organizations. We should closely observe how the experiment evolves in London, where the functional regulators are all in different departments of the same organization.

UNIDENTIFIED MALE [From the Floor]: I wonder why everybody has forgotten the savings and loan business. Those are institutions. Some of them had a lot of capital and the benign neglect in that area cost the U.S. citizens a hell of a lot more money than the regulation of the markets will ever cost.

O'HARA: Let's have our panelists get in one last word.

PATRIKIS: Our discussion did not get into enforcement and the lack of de facto due process with institutions like the SEC and the Federal Reserve. Few, if any, honorable institutions that make a mistake, have the stomach to fight an agency where there is a bona fide disagreement as to jurisdiction or whether a violation exists. That is how powerful regulation is in the United States. There is de jure due process, but there is no de facto due process. If you are an institution that has integrity, it's an issue of "how much does it cost to get out of this problem."

COLBY: Much more important than market structure, is the ability for some firms and some people to play the margins of regulation and play the gaps, and get a major business advantage over other people. Sometimes you

[113] According to the New York Stock Exchange's Shareownership 2000 report, in 1998 there were 84 million shareholders in the United States, with shareholder defined as individuals owning stock directly, through mutual funds, retirement saving accounts or defined contribution pension plans.

[114] The Financial Services Authority, or FSA (previously known as the Securities and Investments Board, SIB), is a single regulatory agency that is responsible for supervising banks, listed money market institutions, and clearing houses in the United Kingdom.

have to think whether the drawback is regulation itself. Can you justify it anymore? Some people are able to take advantage of other people because the other people are more highly regulated.

Part of what we did in ATS was actually more deregulatory than regulatory. There was an imbalance between unregulated broker/dealers and highly regulated exchanges. It wasn't a stable dynamic. So you had to look to see whether you had to have some pieces, or you should have a part of each, but allow them all to compete on a lower regulated basis. That is what Reg. ATS tried to do.

KWALWASSER: I think that we have to constantly make sure that our regulations are appropriate to the markets that we are in. But I think that, as Brandon says, regulation is still a long-term business.

LEE: I strongly agree with Brandon's predictions about the two areas of regulation in the future. But I suggest a third area, which is that the cost of regulating market structure will become much more apparent. That might appear in a hundred different ways. You may get a flight of capital to Europe. Or, there may be other ways in which you see the costs of regulation appearing. That will put pressure to separate, difficult though it may be, the wholesale and the retail ends.

BECKER: First, I agree completely with Ernie Patrikis about the de facto abuse of due process. I would only add to his comments that there is also difficulty in dealing with SROs in a disciplinary context. The position is one where the only person who is willing to go to the mat is the person who has nothing to lose. If you're representing a reputable firm, you are always looking for a way out because you can't risk your reputation with that SRO or government agency.

Second, individual investor participation in the U.S. market is special and will create a demand for different kinds of regulation and fairness.

Third, there is a concern regarding marginal competitors. I deal with the issues of start-ups and new companies. The cost that I feel most directly is the cost of regulatory delay. There can be death by a thousand cuts, as you spend all your venture money trying to get up and running. Regulatory delay is a very real cost that needs to be addressed.

ADKINS: Living day-to-day in a world where my enforcement and legal decisions are subject to real time challenge, I'm somewhat mystified about this talk of people who are afraid of challenge, of SROs. I think there is both de facto and tons of du jour due process. In fact, maybe too much du jour due process. It stuns me to hear people suggest, at least at an SRO level, that there is the fear to challenge, because it happens a lot, which is good.

I absolutely agree that the costs of regulation can and will be unbundled and made more transparent. That is going to encourage a lot of new exchanges that may have not even been thinking about it, to create lower cost, lower regulated exchanges. That is precisely why I worry that the ultimate effect of the ATS release will be the fragmentation of the regulatory system. Forget about an SRO versus SEC structure. Regulation needs to be consolidated, both with respect to its data, and ultimately with respect to its decision-making. One of the potentially negative effects of unbundling costs will be to put that type of structure under a severe threat. That would not be good.

Participant Biographies

Alden S. Adkins, a member of the District of Columbia Bar, is currently Senior Vice President and General Counsel of the NASD Regulation Inc.'s Office of General Counsel. Prior to these duties, Alden served as Vice President of Strategic Planning and Research for the National Association of Securities Dealers, Inc. (NASD). Alden also served for two years as Director of Internal Review and EEO Director for the NASD.

Prior to joining the NASD, Alden served for 10 years as an Attorney with the U.S. Securities and Exchange Commission. While at the SEC, Alden served as Special Counsel to the Chairman of the SEC; established and served as the first Chief of the Office of Automation and International Markets in the Division of Market Regulation; and held the position of Branch Chief of the NMS and Municipal Securities Branch, Division of Market Regulation.

Alden holds a Bachelor of Arts in Classics (Phi Beta Kappa) from Johns Hopkins University and received his Juris Doctor (magna cum laude) from the Washington College of Law of American University. Alden performed as Adjunct Professor of Law at Georgetown University from 1991 through 1993, teaching a course entitled "Global Securities Markets."

Matthew Andresen has been president and CEO of Island since 1998, overseeing management of the company. Under Mr. Andresen's leadership, Island has evolved into the second-largest electronic network (ECN). In the fourth quarter of 1998, 4.6 billion Nasdaq shares were traded on Island, representing an increase of 31% over the previous quarter and 181% increase over the fourth quarter a year ago. Mr. Andresen is also spearheading Island's recently announced plans to file with the SEC for stock exchange status.

Mr. Andresen began his career on Wall Street in 1993 as an assistant trader on the commodities desk at Lehman Brothers. He joined Datek Securities Corp. in discretionary accounts. Prior to joining Island in 1998, Mr. Andresen was self-employed for a year, trading securities for his own portfolio.

Mr. Andresen holds a B.A. in economics and political science from Duke University in Durham, N.C. A championship fencer, he was an alternate for the 1996 U.S. Olympic Team. At Duke, Mr. Andresen was also a National Champion and All-American in the sport.

The Island ECN, Inc., one of the first alternative trading systems, enables both retail and institutional investors to display and execute orders directly and electronically. Broker-dealers leverage Island's speed, easy access and wide range of order information for the benefit of the individual investor. A pioneer in the alternative trading industry, Island is located on the World Wide Web at www.isld.com and is headquartered in New York City.

James J. Angel specializes in finance, financial markets and market microstructure. His current research focuses on trading strategies and market liquidity. He teaches undergraduate and MBA courses in financial management.

Professor Angel's accomplishments including publishing the first sole-authored *Journal of Finance* article ever written at Georgetown. He has also published in numerous other scholarly journals including *Financial Management, Journal of Portfolio Management, Journal of Applied Corporate Finance*, and the *Journal of Investing*. Professor Angel is the first Georgetown finance professor to be appointed to a National Bureau of Economic Research working group.

"Dr. Jim" has testified before Congress about issues relating to the design of financial markets. In addition, he has been quoted in over 20 newspaper articles and has appeared on radio and television, including the Jim Lehrer News Hour. His work has been cited in scholarly journals ranging from *Journal of Finance to the Yale law Journal*. He has presented and discussed papers at numerous professional conferences including the American Finance Association, the American Economics Association, and the Financial Management Association. Furthermore, he has served as a referee for over half a dozen academic journals.

Douglas Atkin is President and CEO of Instinet Corporation, a wholly-owned subsidiary of Reuters Group PLC, and the world's largest agency brokerage firm. After assuming the presidency of Instinet in 1998, Doug's vision, energy and outspoken commitment to market structure reform gave rise to a new Instinet. The firm, now a major force in the financial industry, is committed to using technology to fundamentally change the rules of engagement in the capital markets to improve the performance of investors and issuers worldwide.

Doug joined Instinet in 1984, and has been instrumental in its overall growth. In 1990, he moved to London to head Instinet's international business. Under his leadership, Instinet entered the world stage by establishing operations in Europe and Asia. Instinet also secured membership in the Paris, Frankfurt, Stockholm, Hong Kong and Tokyo exchanges and opened offices in those regions. In 1999, as President of Instinet, Doug led a consortium of six global brokerages and investment houses that took a majority stake in Tradepoint Financial Networks plc, a screen-based for-profit stock exchange headquartered in London. Since that time, five other global financial firms have joined the consortium. Also in 1999, Instinet invested in Archipelago, a leading US-based electronic communications network specializing in Nasdaq stocks.

To promote efficient capital formation in the US, Instinet invested in W.R. Hambrecht + Co., an entrepreneurial investment bank best known for creating the OpenIPO system, an auction-based method of taking companies public. The two companies, through an international joint venture agreement, are pairing Instinet's global agency brokerage with the OpenIPO system to increase the efficiencies of capital raising in Europe and Asia. In an effort to add breadth to Instinet's global brokerage services, Doug championed some other new business initiatives including the successful 1999 launch of a clearance and settlement business, and the announced mid-year 2000 entry into the fixed income and the retail businesses. Also in 1999, Instinet acquired Lynch, Jones & Ryan, the leading provider of commission recapture programs to plan sponsors as a complement to the company's established global equity trading and research businesses.

Doug is a frequent commentator on CBNC and CNN regarding industry issues. He serves on the Trading Committee of the Securities Industry Association, and on the boards of TIBCO Software Inc., Tradepoint Financial Networks plc, W.R. Hambrecht + Co., Archipelago, and Children First, Inc. In addition, he is a director of the NYC Partnership, and a member of the Young Presidents Organization (YPO) International and the U.S. Council for Competitiveness. In the December 20-27 edition of *New York Magazine*, Doug was selected as one of the Top 50 New Yorkers of 1999 for his prominent role as the leader in the redefinition of the financial marketplace. The Lauri Strauss Leukemia Foundation also honored him at a celebrity concert in Carnegie Hall for outstanding achievement in 1999. Doug is a graduate of Tufts University and holds a BA in Economics and Art History. He is married with two children, and an avid collector of photography.

Timothy Baikie is Director, Global Market Initiatives at the Toronto Stock Exchange and is responsible for analyzing market structure issues from a broad, strategic standpoint, including the market model for the Global Equity Market (GEM). He also assisted in developing the TSE's response to the latest proposal to allow Alternative Trading Systems to operate in Canada. In addition, his duties include assisting the regulatory and business divisions of the Exchange on special projects and market regulation issues. Previously, he was Special Counsel, Market Regulation and Director of the Regulatory and Market Policy Division of the Exchange, which is responsible for policy and rule development for the equities and derivative markets. Before that, he was Manager, Market Policy and Manager of Listed Company Policy and Regulation. He has spoken at numerous conferences on market regulation, market structure and corporate governance issues and was a member of the Advisory Board for the 1999 Canadian Corporate/Securities Law Moot Court Competition. He has received a B.A. from York University (Glendon College), an LL.B. and a B.C.L. from McGill University and an LL.M. from the University of Illinois at Urbana-Champaign. He was called to the Ontario Bar in 1987.

Frank E. Baxter was born in and attended grammar and high school in Northern California. He graduated from the University of California at Berkeley with a BA degree in economics with honors in 1961. Before college he enlisted in the Air Force for four years.

After college he worked at the Bank of California, San Francisco. In 1963 he joined J.S. Strauss and Company, San Francisco which then was a major third market firm.

In 1974 he joined Jefferies and Company, Inc. as a salesman in their Los Angeles office. In 1975 he moved to New York to manage the New York office and become a director of the firm. In 1983 he was made National Sales Manager. In 1985 he opened and managed the London office. On January 1, 1986 he became President and Chief Operating Officer. On March 19, 1987 he was made Chief Executive Officer, serving in that capacity through 2000. In September of 1990 was made Chairman.

Mr. Baxter also holds the following positions:

Director, Investment Technology Group

Affiliate Member, LA Security Financial Analysts

Director, National Association of Securities Dealers

Director, Nasdaq

Trustee, I Have A Dream Foundation, LA Chapter
Director, Los Angeles Opera
Dean's CEO Advisory Committee, Marshall School of Business
Director, Pacific Research Institute
Trustee, University of California, Berkeley Foundation
Trustee, Los Angeles County Museum of Art

He is a member of the Los Angeles Country Club, Los Angeles; Wilshire Country Club, Los Angeles; The Regency Club, Los Angeles; Siwanoy Country Club, Bronxville, New York and the University Club, New York City.

He has been married to Katherine since 1962 and they have three children, Stacey, Matthew, and Katherine. They have three grandchildren – Vanessa, Nicholas, and Theresa.

Mr. Baxter is a marathon runner, plays golf, tennis and enjoys the opera and skiing.

Brandon Becker advises and represents clients on broker-dealer regulatory issues, related issues affecting other financial market participants and other matters involving capital markets issues such as derivative trading. He is the former Director of the SEC's Division of Market Regulation and served as a staff member of the President's Working Group on Financial Markets as well as the CFTC's Financial Products Advisory Committee. Mr. Becker has taught courses on Corporations, Securities Regulation, Broker-Dealer Regulation and Global Securities Markets at a variety of law schools. Education: University of Minnesota, B.A. 1974; University of San Diego, J.D. 1977; Columbia University, LL.M. 1979.

Alfred R. Berkeley, III, was appointed Vice Chairman of the Board of Directors of The Nasdaq Stock Market, Inc., on July 27, 2000. Since 1996, Berkeley had served as President of Nasdaq®. As Vice Chairman, he continues his long-standing and successful efforts to both build Nasdaq and to communicate its values and strategies to the leading existing and potential issuers.

Prior to joining Nasdaq, he was a Managing Director and Senior Banker in the Corporate Finance Department of Alex. Brown & Sons Incorporated, financing computer software and electronic commerce companies.

Berkeley joined Alex. Brown & Sons in 1972 as a research analyst. He became a general partner of Alex. Brown in 1983. From 1985 to 1987, he served as Head of Information Services for the firm. In that capacity, he was responsible for all corporate information services, including both the firm's back and front office technology. Berkeley then moved to Alex. Brown's

Merger and Acquisition department where, from 1987 to 1989, he developed the firm's technology practice.

Berkeley served as a captain in the United States Air Force from 1968 to 1972. He is a graduate of The Wharton School at the University of Pennsylvania (M.B.A., 1968) and the University of Virginia (B.A., 1966)

Berkeley is married and has three daughters. The family resides in Baltimore, Maryland.

Robert L.D. Colby. As Deputy Director of the Securities and Exchange Commission's Division of Market Regulation, Robert L.D. Colby is responsible for the regulation and oversight of securities firms, clearing organizations, and the United States securities markets.

Mr. Colby was named Deputy Director in September 1993. Previously, Mr. Colby was Chief Counsel of the Division, and Branch Chief of the Division's office of Market Structure.

Mr. Colby received his Law degree, cum laude, from Harvard Law School in 1981. He earned his Bachelor of Arts degree, summa cum laude, from Bowdoin College in 1977. He has authored articles on the national market system, broker-dealer regulation, and other subjects, and has served as an Adjunct Professor with the Georgetown University Law Center.

Mike Cormack is manager, Equity Trading, for American Century Investments, the investment manager of a diversified family of mutual funds and institutional accounts. The company is headquartered in Kansas City, Missouri.

Mr. Cormack oversees the domestic equity trading area that handles trading for the company's portfolio management groups in Kansas City; Mountain View, California; and Greenwich, Connecticut. Previously, he was a senior equity trader for American Century. Mr. Cormack joined the company in 1991.

Mr. Cormack holds a bachelor's degree in economics from The Johns Hopkins University. He is co-head of the executive committee for the Financial Information Exchange (FIX) – an emerging electronic communications standard in the global financial marketplace. Mr. Cormack is also a member of the Nasdaq Quality of Markets Committee.

Paul Davis is co-head of the Quantitative Portfolio Management and Trading department. He joined TIAA-CREF in 1983 after working at Prudential-Bache Securities. He graduated from West Virginia University and has a doctorate in mathematics from Carnegie Mellon University. He has taught mathematics at Lehigh University, Manhattanville College and West Virginia University.

TIAA-CREF is a leading, national, non-profit financial services organization serving the general public, and is also the premier pension system for people employed in education and research in the U.S. It offers high-quality, low-cost mutual funds, annuities, IRAs, insurance, and trust services, and also manages several state-sponsored college financing programs. The TIAA-CREF pension system ranks as the world's largest, based on assets under management. In total, the organization manages almost $300 billion. TIAA-CREF is headquartered in New York City, with regional offices throughout the United States.

Ian Domowitz is the Mary Jean and Frank P. Smeal Professor of Finance at the Smeal College of Business Administration, Pennsylvania State University. He received his Ph.D. in Economics from the University of California in 1982. He previously taught in the Economics Department and in the Kellogg Graduate School of Management, Northwestern University, and was a member of the research faculty of the Institute for Policy Research at Northwestern. Other positions have included that of visiting scholar at Cornell University, and research associate, Center for the Study of Futures Markets, Columbia University

Professor Domowitz's areas of expertise include Finance, Econometrics, Statistics, and Industrial Organization, including work on the organization and regulation of trading market structures. Research and publication in these areas have been supported by the Alfred P. Sloan Foundation and the National Science Foundation. He is a consultant to various government and international organizations, including the Federal Reserve System, the Commodity Futures Trading Commission, the International Monetary Fund, and the World Bank, as well as to various securities exchanges. He serves as chair of the Scientific Advisory Board of ITG, Inc. A former member of the NASD's Bond Market Transparency Committee, he currently is chair of the Economic Advisory Board of Nasdaq.

Kevin Foley manages U.S. electronic trading products at Bloomberg Financial Markets and is President of Bloomberg Tradebook LLC, an electronic broker of equities for institutional investors and for other brokerage firms. Mr. Foley has been with Bloomberg for nine years. During this time he oversaw the development of many popular Bloomberg products for the analysis of fixed income and equity securities. He has also served as regional sales manager of Bloomberg's team of applications specialists. He helped launch and served as an editor of Bloomberg Magazine. He began his career at Bloomberg as a fixed income specialist.

Before joining Bloomberg he traded U.S. government bonds for Drexel Burnham Lambert in New York. He received an M.B.A in Finance from Columbia University in 1987. He is married to Dr. Donna Silbert, a psychotherapist in private practice. Thy have a two-year-old son, Bennett Cornelius, and are expecting a second child in May. They live in New York City and West Cornwall, CT.

Buzzy Geduld is the President and CEO of Herzog Heine Geduld, and has been with the firm for over 30 years. Herzog Heine Geduld, a Merrill Lynch company, is a leading market maker in more than 10,000 securities. The firm is a member of the New York Stock Exchange and other leading Exchanges.

Buzzy Geduld was born in Brooklyn and is currently living in New York City. He serves on the Board of Directors of the Starlight Foundation, is a board member of the Wall Street Chapter of St. Jude Children's Research and he is a member the SIA Trading Committee. He has served on the Board of Directors of Nasdaq, Inc., the NASD *Quality of Markets Committee,* the Board of Governors of the Security Traders Association, is a past President, Director, Vice President and Secretary of STANY, past President of STANY *Gratuity Fund* and has served on the trading committee of the NASD.

Employment History: Herzog Heine Geduld, 04/98 President and CEO, 12/86 President, 09/76 Senior Vice President – Trading, 10/68 Vice President and Trader.

Allan Grody is President of Financial InterGroup and Adjunct Professor, Stern School of Business. Mr. Grody has been a consultant and advisor to the world's largest financial institutions and exchanges including the world's first electronic exchange. He was a Partner and founder of Coopers & Lybrand's Financial Industry Consulting Practice, founded and teaches NYU's graduate course in Risk Management Systems and guest lectures on financial markets, financial systems and venture capital investing. He is based in New York City.

William R. Harts is Managing Director of the Global Direct Equity Markets Group at Salomon Smith Barney Inc. This position includes responsibility for the firm's strategic investments as well as market structure developments relating to equity trading. Before taking on his current duties, Mr. Harts was co-head of the firm's Global Portfolio Trading operation, with responsibility for desks in New York, London and Tokyo. He came to SSB in September 1993 from Lehman Brothers where he established an automated market-making and trading operation for the Worldwide Equities Division. Prior to that, he worked at Goldman, Sachs & Co. for almost four years in their Quantitative Strategies Group designing equity derivative risk analysis software and convertible bond trading systems. He has been a featured speaker at several industry forums, including the Institute for International Research's Trade Execution Congress, the Pace University Center for the Study of Equity Markets' Securities Industry Conference, and a panelist at the Baruch College Zicklin School of Business' Regulation of U.S. Equity Markets Conference.

Mr. Harts served as Vice Chairman of the Philadelphia Stock Exchange from 1996 through 1999; he has been a member of that exchange since 1994. He is a member of the Boston, Chicago and Pacific Stock Exchanges. He is a member of the Board of Directors of Primex Trading.

Before coming to Wall Street, Mr. Harts worked in the computer industry for more than twelve years and is the author of a best selling data communications software package. His writings on various aspects of the computer industry have been published internationally in PC Magazine. As a management consultant his clients included AT&T, NCR and American Airlines.

He lives in Bedford, New York with his wife Susan, daughter Eleni and son Sam. He has recently served on the board of the Northern Westchester Center for the Arts.

Diana Henriques joined The New York Times in October 1989 as a financial reporter after having been a writer for Barron's National Business and Financial Weekly, a Dow Jones publication, since July 1986. Since joining The Times, she has specialized in reporting on financial fraud, white-collar crime and corporate governance issues.

She was a member of a team that won the 1999 Gerald R. Loeb Award for deadline reporting, in the large newspaper division, for coverage of the near-collapse of Longterm Capital Management, a hedge fund whose troubles rocked the financial markets in September 1998. She was also one of four reporters honored for a 1996 series on how wealthy Americans can legally side-step taxes; the four reporters were finalists, in the large newspaper division, of the 1996 Gerald R. Loeb Award, and were winners of the large newspaper division prize for investigative reporting awarded by the Deadline Club, the New York City chapter of Sigma Delta Chi, the Society of Professional Journalists.

While at Barron's, Ms. Henriques handled news and feature assignments that spanned the financial scene, from precious metals to corporate profiles; her investigative reporting uncovered a variety of investor fraud and shareholder abuses in both the U.S. and the Canadian markets. She was a finalist in the magazine division of the 1987 Loeb awards for her examination of the explosive growth in the world's gold supply.

From August 1982 to June 1986, Ms. Henriques was a business writer for the Philadelphia Inquirer, covering public finance and economic issues in the U.S. and abroad. In January 1985, she began covering Wall Street as The Inquirer's New York financial correspondent.

From 1976 to 1981, Ms. Henriques worked as an investigative reporter and state government reporter for The Trenton (N.J.) Times. Her articles about the state's housing finance agency, Economic Development Authority and state prison medical system prompted several criminal prosecutions and statewide reforms. She was awarded the New Jersey Bell Prize for Enterprise Reporting in 1977.

From 1974 to 1976, she worked as a copy editor for the Palo Alto (Calif.) Times, and from 1971 to 1974 as a local and state government reporter for the Asbury Park Press (N.J.).

Born on December 17, 1948 in Bryan, Texas, Ms. Henriques is a 1969 graduate of George Washington University, Washington, D.C. She graduated with distinction, Phi Beta Kappa, majored in International Affairs and was a General Motors Scholar. She now serves as a member of the International Advisory Council of the university's Elliott School of International Affairs.

Ms. Henriques is the author of "The Machinery of Greed: Public Authority Abuse and What to Do About It," published by Lexington Books, 1986; and of "Fidelity's World: The Secret Life and Public Power of the Mutual Fund Giant," published by Scribners, 1995. Her latest book, "The White Sharks of Wall Street: Thomas Mellon Evans and the Original Corporate Raiders," was published by Scribners in May.

Ms. Henriques is a frequent lecturer for the American Press Institute in Reston, Va., and is a member of Investigative Reporters and Editors (IRE). She is married and lives in Hoboken, New Jersey.

Greg Ip is a Senior Special Writer at The Wall Street Journal. Until January 2001, he covered stock market trends and developments in securities market structure for the Journal's Money and Investing section. Since January, he has covered the Federal Reserve and the economy in the Journal's Washington Bureau. Greg joined the Journal in 1996. Before that, he worked for six years in Toronto at the Financial Post and later The Globe and Mail as a business and economics reporters. He graduated from Carleton University in Ottawa, Canada in 1989 with an honors BA in journalism and economics.

William R. Johnston, was named president, chief operating officer, and a member of the office of the chief executive at the New York Stock Exchange in July 1996.

Mr. Johnston's responsibilities include overseeing the areas of new listings and client service: operations, equities, market data and technology; regulation; and the office of the general counsel.

Prior to his current position, Mr. Johnston had been vice chairman and director of the NYSE and a senior managing director of LaBranche & Co., a leading specialist firm. He joined LaBranche & Co. in 1990, having previously been chairman and chief executive officer of Agora Securities, Inc., the company he founded in 1980. He also served as senior vice president and director of Mitchum, Jones & Templeton, Inc., from October 1971 to August 1980.

A member of the NYSE since 1964, Mr. Johnston was named as a director of the Exchange in 1992 and vice chairman in 1995. From 1991 until 1992, he was a senior floor official, and previously served as floor governor from 1985 to 1991 and floor official from 1979 to 1985.

Since 1985, he served on the Exchange's Quality of Markets Committee, the Market Performance Committee, the Human Resources Policy and Compensation committee, the Financial operational Surveillance Committee, the Institutional Traders Advisory Committee and the Floor Facilities Committee. In addition, Mr. Johnston serves on the NYSE Foundation Board of Directors.

Mr. Johnston is president and director of the Floor Members Outreach Program, Inc., and treasurer and director of the Cancer Research & Treatment Fund, where he has been a member of the board for over 15 years. He is a member of the Board of Trustees of Washington and Lee University, from which he graduated in 1961 with a B.S. in Commerce. He is married and has two children.

Raymond L. Killian, Jr. holds the positions of Chairman, President and Chief Executive Officer of ITG Inc., an NASD registered Broker/Dealer, and of Investment Technology Group, Inc., the holding company (Nasdaq symbol: ITGI) which owns 100% of ITG Inc.

ITG Inc. was incorporated in September 1991, and became a registered Broker/Dealer with the NASD in March 1992. Prior to ITG's incorporation, Mr. Killian ran the group as a department within Jefferies & Company, Inc., a subsidiary of Jefferies Group, Inc. (Nasdaq symbol: JEFG).

From 1985 through 1990, Mr. Killian served as Executive Vice President and National Sales Manager of Jefferies & Company, Inc. Responsibilities included all areas of sales and marketing for the brokerage. In addition, Mr.

Killian served as a member of the Board of Directors of Jefferies Group through February 1998.

Mr. Killian is a graduate of Boston University, with a BS in Education. Professional affiliations include:

Member, Boston Securities Traders Association

Past Member of the Executive Committee, National Organization of Investment Professionals (NOIP)

Past Governor, Boston Stock Exchange

President of the Board of Trustees, Cotting School, Inc.

Member of the Global Investment Technology Leadership Roundtable

Edward A. Kwalwasser, was named group executive vice president and a member of the office of the chief executive at the New York Stock Exchange in June 1995. Mr. Kwalwasser is responsible for member firm regulation, market surveillance, enforcement, market structure, government relations and regulatory support.

He had been executive vice president, regulation since September 1990, when he was also named to the Exchange' s management committee. Mr. Kwalwasser had been senior vice president, regulatory group, since August 1989, and was named senior vice president, member firm regulation in June 1985. He joined the NYSE in 1984 as senior vice president, regulatory quality review.

Before joining the NYSE, Mr. Kwalwasser held several positions with the Securities and Exchange Commission in Washington, D.C. He jointed the agency in 1967 and was named chief regulatory attorney and assistant regional administrator of the SEC's Washington regional office before becoming associate director for the SEC's division of market regulation.

A native of New York City, he earned a B.B.A degree in economics from the City College of New York in 1962 and a Law degree from Cornell University in 1965.

Ruben Lee is the Director of the Oxford Finance Group, a research and consulting firm. From 1989 to 1992 he was a Fellow of Nuffield College, Oxford University, where he specialized in financial economics and law. From 1980 to 1984 he worked in the capital markets in New York and London for Salomon Brothers International. Dr. Lee is the author of a newly published book entitled "What is an Exchange? The Automation, Management, and Regulation of Financial Markets" (Oxford University Press), and many other publications and articles. He has lectured and consulted throughout the world, most recently in many parts of Asia. This work has included being Chief of Party of the USAID team on Capital

Markets Development in Kyrgyzstan, advising the Korean Government on Inter-Market Competition and Self-Regulation, and preparing a report for the OECD on "The Development of Capital Markets in Central Asia."

William A. Lupien established OptiMark, Inc. in 1996, with a mandate to improve the structure and operational capabilities of the securities market. Mr. Lupien is co-inventor of OptiMark's patented trading technology, a revolutionary method of structuring markets for securities and other fungible items.

Mr. Lupien has been active in the securities industry since joining the California-based brokerage firm of Mitchum, Jones & Templeton, Inc. (MJT), in 1965. Mr. Lupien served as chairman and CEO of MJT, while also a specialist on the floor of the Pacific Stock Exchange for 17 years. He was a Nasdaq market-maker for 5 years.

Upon leaving MJT in 1983, Mr. Lupien served as president, then chairman and CEO of Instinet Corporation, and was responsible for Instinet's move into trading Nasdaq stocks. During Mr. Lupien's tenure, Instinet's trading volumes increased tenfold, its revenues increased seventeen-fold, and the company was acquired by Reuters Plc.

In addition to his work within the securities industry, Mr. Lupien has served on numerous private and public company boards, including a current position as Trustee of the Securities Industry Institute. Mr. Lupien is a graduate of San Diego State University.

Mr. Lupien's interests include horseback riding, fly fishing, photography, the history of the American West, music, travel, art, and gardening.

Peter B. Madoff is Senior Managing Director of Bernard L. Madoff Investment Securities. Mr. Madoff's past services include Vice Chairman of the NASD Board of Governors, as well as having served on the Executive Committee and Board of Governors of Nasdaq. He is also a past president of the Securities Traders Association of New York (STANY) and past Chairman of the NASD District 10 Business Conduct Committee.

He presently serves as a member of the Board of Governors and Executive Committee of the Cincinnati Stock Exchange and is a member of the NASD Industry Advisory Committee for Technology (IAC).

Peter is a graduate of Queens College and the Fordham Law School and is a member of the Bar of the State of New York.

Michael Murphy joined First Union Securities in April 2000 to lead the Equity Trading efforts for the firm. In his current role, Mr. Murphy manages a trading floor of more than 75 professionals.

Prior to joining First Union, Mr. Murphy worked on the buyside as a founding partner of Kern Capital Management and as Head of Trading for Morgan Grenfell Asset Management. Mr. Murphy was also a former partner with Alex Brown where he was Head of Trading.

Mr. Murphy is a frequent guest on numerous financial networks including CNBC, CNN and CNNfn. He currently serves on the Upstairs Trading Advisory Committee for the New York Stock Exchange. Mr. Murphy previously served two 4-year terms on the Institutional Trading Advisory Committee for the NYSE and several advisory committees for the NASD. He was a former Chair of the Security Traders Association.

Mr. Murphy received his B.A. from West Virginia University. He currently resides in Baltimore, MD with his three daughters.

Jeanne L. Murtaugh is Vice Chairman of BNY ESI & Co., the successor to ESI Securities Company. She has held this position since 1991 and has been a director of the company since 1988. Prior to that, she was Vice President of Morgan Stanley & Company in 1987. From 1973 to 1984, Ms. Murtaugh served in various management positions at Morgan Guaranty Trust and Wachovia Bank & Trust, where she established the Bank's retail brokerage business and global custody services.

Ms. Murtaugh is responsible for strategic and business planning for BNY ESI's institutional business. She played a pivotal role in the firm's development of one of the first "STP" trading environments in 1989. Most recently, her focus on the strategic direction of ESI led to the firm's acquisition by the Bank of New York at the end of 1997.

ESI, is one of the top-tier institutional agency brokerage firms in the United States. In addition to their trading proficiency, ESI is also a leading provider of innovative technology supporting trade management, information networks, and the integration of applications, systems, and networks into a seamless process.

Ms. Murtaugh has been a frequent guest speaker on industry strategy and related technologies at numerous conferences, including the ABA Annual Conference, Institutional Investor's Trader Forum, the Stratus & Tandem Conferences, and the Security Industries Conference.

Ms. Murtaugh earned a Bachelor of Science Degree from the University of North Carolina and attended the Executive Program at the Kenen-Flager School at Chapel Hill.

Maureen O'Hara is the Robert W. Purcell Professor of Finance at Cornell's Johnson Graduate School of Management. Her research and teaching interest are in the area of market microstructure, which focuses on the role and structure of securities markets. Some recent research topics include the impact of transparency on inter-market competitiveness, the effects of order preferencing on market pricing behaviour, and the optimal regulation of exchanges and alternative trading systems. She is the author of Market Microstructure Theory, which was published by Blackwell in 1995, and she is the Executive Editor of the Review of Financial Studies. Professor O'Hara has served as President of the Western Finance Association, a leading international organization of financial economists, as a member of the Nasdaq Economic Advisory Board, and she is currently Vice President of the American Finance Association.

Arthur J. Pacheco, 52, is Senior Managing Director and Product Manager for the Equity Division of Bear Stearns, was former President and CEO of STRIKE Technologies LLC, an Electronic Communications Network/Alternative Trading System based in New York.

With over 36 years of experience in Nasdaq/Over-the-Counter sales and trading, Mr. Pacheco has also been a Senior Managing Director and Co-manager of the Over-the-Counter Trading Department of Bear Stearns & Co., Inc., in addition to being manager of Over-the-Counter Institutional Sales. Mr. Pacheco joined Bear Stearns in 1989 and was promoted to Senior Managing Director in 1991.

Prior to joining Bear Stearns, Mr. Pacheco was Manager of Over-the-Counter trading at Cantor Fitzgerald.

Mr. Pacheco presently serves on the Executive Advisory Committee of The Security Traders Association, the Board of Directors of The National Organization of Investment Professionals and on the Board of Directors for 5th Market Inc., a company presently focused on building transaction hubs in markets with complex underlying trading methodologies. He is on the Board of Directors for JAYWALK.COM, a web accessible provider of independent investment research. Previously, Mr. Pacheco has also been Chairman of the Security Traders Association and President of the Security Traders Association of New York.

Mr. Pacheco is the Chairman of The One to One Foundation and The Wall Street Charity Fund. He is also a member of the Advisory Committee of the Foundation for Teaching Entrepreneurship and a member of the Board of Trustees of Landmark College, which is located in Putney, Vermont and is the only accredited college for students with Attention Deficit Disorder in the U.S. He is also contributing patron of the Metropolitan Opera and the National Arts Club.

Mr. Pacheco resides in Holmdel, New Jersey with his wife, Jeanne Marie, and their three children.

Aldo Parcesepe is a 30-year veteran in the securities industry. He began his career in 1968 as an apprentice in Bear Stearns' equity order room, and in 1971 he accepted the position of equity trader at Allen & Co., Inc. until returning to Bear Stearns in 1979 as a senior position trader. In 1987, Aldo was promoted to manager of OTC trading, and soon thereafter was named Senior Managing Director of Bear Stearns & Co., Inc. which position he occupies today. Aldo is a past member of the NASD Trading Committee and is presently a member of the S.I.A. Trading Committee. He has served the industry through various committees and forums sponsored by S.T.A.N.Y. and the Security Traders Association, and he has acted as a senior industry spokesman to regulators and legislators.

Ernest T. Patrikis is Special Advisor to AIG Chairman M.R. Greenberg.

Mr. Patrikis joined AIG in 1998 following a 30-year career with the Federal Reserve Bank of New York, where he was First Vice President, the Bank's second ranking officer. In addition to his position as First Vice President, Mr. Patrikis also served as an alternate member of the Federal Open Market Committee, the Federal Reserve's monetary policymaking group.

Earlier in his career, he held positions as General Counsel and Executive Vice President at the Bank. He also served as Deputy General Counsel of the Federal Open Market Committee for five years.

Mr. Patrikis has served as a member of the staff of the President's Working Group on Financial Markets and as a member of the Committee on Payments and Settlement Systems of the G-10 central bank governors.

Mr. Patrikis holds a J.D. degree from Cornell Law School and a B.A. degree from the University of Massachusetts. He is a member of the American and New York State Bar Associations and the Association of the Bar of the City of New York. Mr. Patrikis is a Vice Chair of the International Practice Section of the New York State Bar Association, and he is a member of the Securities Law Committee of the Association of the Bar. He also chairs the Ad Hoc Y2K Task Force for the Association of the Bar.

Additionally, Mr. Patrikis is a member of the advisory committee of the Business Council for the United Nations and a member of the advisory council of the Morin Center for Banking and Financial Law Studies at Boston University Law School. He is also a member of the Council on Foreign Relations and a fellow of the Foreign Policy Association.

Junius W. Peake is the Monfort Distinguished Professor of Finance at the University of Northern Colorado. He was a former Governor and Vice-

Chairman of the National Association of Securities Dealers, Inc. He has been a featured speaker at the Wharton School of the University of Pennsylvania, the Amos Tuck School at Dartmouth, Northwestern University, the University of Chicago, the University of Memphis, and the Leonard Stern School of New York University, and is quoted regularly in publications such as the Wall Street Journal, the Financial Times (London), Business Week, Forbes, and U.S. News and World Report. He has also appeared on national television on business programs of CNN, CNBC, CBS and WWOR-TV. Professor Peake has been invited a number of times to give expert testimony before committees of the U.S. Senate and House of Representatives, as well as before the Securities & Exchange Commission. He writes a regular column for the Denver Business Journal.

Gerald Putnam is the founder and Chief Executive Officer of Archipelago Holdings, originally a joint venture with software developer, Townsend Analytics. Since its inception, Archipelago has offered subscribers outbound order preferencing to effectively create a national limit order book for Nasdaq stocks and soon Listed stocks. Jerry has attracted major investors to the ECN from both the institutional and retail financial services sectors. Under Jerry's leadership, Archipelago has more than tripled its daily share volume in 1999 and has more than doubled its volume in 2000 through the 3rd quarter. In July 2000, through their alliance, Archipelago and the Pacific Exchange files rules with the SEC to create the first totally open, fully electronic U.S. stock exchange.

Jerry has developed a deep understanding of the securities industry through his involvement in institutional and derivative sales at several major brokerage firms in New York and Chicago since 1983. He was at Walsh, Greenwood from 1983 to 1987, and moved to Chicago in 1985 to open their institutional sales desk. From there, he gained further experience at Jefferies & Company, PaineWebber, Prudential and Geldermann Securities, Inc. Moving into the electronic trading arena in 1994, Jerry founded Terra Nova, an on-line broker dealer, and was its president until January 1999. He currently serves on Terra Nova's Board of Directors.

Jerry received a Bachelor of Science degree in economics with a major in accounting from the University of Pennsylvania, Wharton School in 1981. During January 2000, he was inducted into the Entrepreneurship Hall of Fame sponsored by the University of Illinois at Chicago. Jerry is married and 41 years old.

Evan Schulman is a co-founder of Upstream Technologies, designing software to generate more efficient portfolios for the retail investor, either directly or through financial planners and brokers. He also co-founded Lattice Trading, recently acquired by State Street Bank. He is the author of articles for several publications, including the Journal of Portfolio Management, the Financial Analysts Journal, The Canadian Investment Review and the Encyclopedia of Investments.

His work has been the subject of three case studies at the Graduate School of Business at Harvard University; his career is the subject matter of Chapter 9 of Alan Reubenfeld's *Super Traders,* Probus Press, 1992.

Evan is a New Englander by choice, having emigrated from Canada. He has adopted the New England tradition early and enthusiastically, becoming a cranberry farmer in the process.

Robert A. Schwartz is Marvin M. Speiser Professor of Finance and University Distinguished Professor in the Zicklin School of Business, Baruch College, CUNY. Before joining the Baruch faculty in 1997, he was Professor of Finance and Economics and Yamaichi Faculty Fellow at New York University's Leonard N. Stern School of Business, where he had been a member of the faculty since 1965. Professor Schwartz received his Ph.D. in Economics from Columbia University. His research is in the area of financial economics, with a primary focus on the structure of securities markets. He has published numerous journal articles and seven books, including *Reshaping the Equity Markets: A Guide for the 1990s,* Harper Business, 1991 (reissued by Business One Irwin, 1993). He is a co-chairman of the recently formed Security Traders Institute. He has also served as a consultant to various market centers including the New York Stock Exchange, the American Stock Exchange, the National Association of Securities Dealers, Instinet, the Arizona Stock Exchange, Deutsche Börse, and the Bolsa Mexicana. From April 1983 to April 1988, he was an associate editor of *The Journal of Finance*, and he is currently an associate editor of the *Review of Quantitative Finance and Accounting* and the *Review of Pacific Basin Financial Markets and Policies* and is a member of the advisory board of *International Finance.* In December 1995, Professor Schwartz was named the first chairman of Nasdaq's Economic Advisory Board, and he served on the EAB until Spring 1999.

Erik R. Sirri is the Chief Economist of the United States Securities and Exchange Commission. He serves as the senior advisor to the Commission and its Chairman on major economic policy issues. He also heads the Office of Economic Analysis, which is responsible for assisting the Commission in establishing regulatory policy and for evaluating the economic impact of proposed Commission actions on the capital markets.

Before joining the Commission, he was Assistant Professor of Finance at the Harvard Business School from 1989 to 1995 and is currently on leave as an Associate Professor of Finance at Babson College. Sirri received his B.S. in Astronomy from the California Institute of Technology in 1979, an M.B.A. from the University of California, Irvine, in 1984, and his Ph.D. in Finance from the University of California, Los Angeles, in 1990. Before becoming a professor, he worked on planetary astronomy missions for NASA and on space surveillance sensors in the aerospace industry. He has consulted for investment banks, proprietary trading firms, brokerage houses, economic consulting firms, and mutual fund companies. Sirri has also authored numerous academic articles, book chapters, and business school cases.

Holly Stark manages Kern Capital Management's trading desk and is responsible for developing execution strategies designed to maximize returns while minimizing transaction costs. Prior to joining Kern Capital Management in 2000, Holly was with Dalton, Greiner, Hartman, Maher & Co. (DGHM) for ten years where she was responsible for all trading activities. For eight years prior to DGHM, Holly was with Dillon, Read Capital, Inc., the predecessor firm to DGHM. Through her current and past participation on advisory committees at the NASD, New York Stock Exchange and The Investment Company Institute, Holly is actively involved with the changing structure of today's capital markets. Holly earned her Bachelor of Arts from Rutgers College in 1978.

Benn Steil is Senior Fellow and holder of the Linda J. Wachner Chair in Foreign Economic Policy at the Council on Foreign Relations in New York. He is also the Editor of *International Finance* (Blackwell Publishers), a member of the European Shadow Financial Regulatory Committee, and a member of the Advisory Board of the European Capital Markets Institute. Until November 1998, he was Director of the International Economics Programme at the Royal Institute of International Affairs in London. Prior to his appointment at the Institute in 1992, he held a Lloyd's of London Tercentenary Research Fellowship at Nuffield College, Oxford, where he received his PhD in Economics.

Dr. Steil has written and spoken widely on securities trading and market regulation. His research and market commentary are regularly covered in publications such as the *Financial Times, Wall Street Journal, New York Times, International Herald Tribune, USA Today, The Economist, Barrons, Business Week, Fortune, Time, Newsweek, Financial News, Securities Industry News,* and Reuters and Bloomberg online. Among his books are a critically acclaimed study of *The European Equity Markets*, a major text on

Institutional Investors, and an edited volume on cross-border antitrust (*Antitrust Goes Global*). Dr Steil has also worked for investment banks in New York and London, in systems analysis and foreign exchange, and currently provides consultancy services to exchanges, securities houses and government bodies around the world.

Hans R. Stoll is The Anne Marie and Thomas B. Walker, Jr., Professor of Finance and Director of the Financial Markets Research Center at the Owen Graduate School of Management, Vanderbilt University, Nashville, Tennessee, 37203. He came to Vanderbilt in 1980 from the Wharton School of the University of Pennsylvania where he had been a faculty member since 1966. He received an A.B. degree from Swarthmore College in 1961 an M.B.A. and Ph.D. degrees from the Graduate School of Business of the University of Chicago in 1963 and 1966, respectively.

He has published several books and more than 60 articles on subjects including the forward foreign exchange market, options, commodity futures, small business financing, the impact of institutional investors on the stock market, regulation of securities markets, the theory of dealers in securities markets, the law of one price in international commodity markets, the new option markets, the small firm effect, stock index futures, stock market structure and volatility, the Nasdaq market and other subjects. His book, Futures and Options, with Robert Whaley appeared in 1992.

Professor Stoll is best known for developing and testing the put-call parity relation for option prices, for modeling and testing the behaviour of securities markets dealers, for his work on program trading and the "triple witching hour," and for his work on the sources of the bid-ask spread. In 1996 he received the Earl Sutherland Prize, awarded for outstanding research across all fields at Vanderbilt University.

Stoll was a visiting professor at the Board of Governors of the Federal Reserve System in 1968-69, and he served on the staff of the Institutional Investor Study of the Securities and Exchange Commission in 1969-70. In 1976-77 he was a Senior Fulbright-Hays Visiting Lecturer at ESSEC in Paris, France. He has also been a visiting professor at the University of Chicago (1975-76), at the University of Karlsruhe (1986), and at the University of British Columbia (July, 1990).

Professor Stoll is president-elect of the American Finance Association, and he will become president of the association in 1999. He has also served as president of the Western Finance Association. He has been a director of the American Finance Association, the Financial Management Association, and the Institute for the Study of Security Markets. He is advisory editor of the Journal of Financial Markets. He is an Associate Editor of the Journal of

Financial Economics, The Journal of Finance, The Journal of Financial and Quantitative Analysis, The Journal of Derivatives, Review of Derivatives Research, The Review of Futures Markets, Financial Management, The Journal of Financial Research, the European Finance Review, and The Journal of Financial Intermediation.

Stoll has served on various government and industry advisory panels, including the Quality of Markets Committee of the NASD, formed to study the crash of 1987, and the advisory panel of the Office of Technology Assessment, formed to oversee a study of securities markets technology. He has been a member of the Shadow Securities and Exchange Commission. He has served as a public director of the Futures Industry Association. He serves as a member of the Economic Advisory Board of the NASD. Professor Stoll has been a consultant to various business concerns and government agencies.

Professor Stoll teaches courses in Derivatives Markets, Equities Markets, Investments, International Financial Management and Corporate Finance.

Richard Sylla is the Henry Kaufman Professor of the History of Financial Institutions and Markets and Professor of Economics at the Stern School of Business of New York University. He is also a Research Associate of the National Bureau of Economic Research. He received the B.A. Summa cum laud (1962), the M.A. (1965), and the Ph.D. (1969), all from Harvard University. He is the author of The American Capital Market, 1846-1914(1975), co-author of The Evolution of the American Economy (1993; 1st ed 1980) and, with the late Sidney Homer, A History of Interest Rates, 3rd ed. (1991), and co-editor of Patterns of European Industrialization – The Nineteenth Century (1991), The State, the Financial System, and Economic Modernization (1999), and of journal articles, essays, and reviews in economics and economics history. He is a former editor of The Journal of Economics History, and in 2000-2001 is president of the Economic History Association. Current research focus: Financial development of the U.S., especially the early decades.

Richard F. Syron is Chairman of the Board and Chief Executive Officer of Thermo Electron Corporation. Thermo Electron Corporation is a global leader in providing technology-based instruments, components, and systems that offer total solutions for markets ranging from life sciences to telecommunications to food and beverage production. In 1999, Thermo Electron's instrument businesses, based in Waltham, Massachusetts, reported $2.2 billion in revenues and employed approximately 14,000 people worldwide.

Mr. Syron has also served as an independent director of Thermo Electron since September 1997. Prior to joining Thermo Electron, Mr. Syron served as the sixteenth Chairman and Chief Executive Officer of the American Stock Exchange since April 1, 1994.

Mr. Syron came to the Amex after more than 20 years in the economic and banking communities. From 1989 to 1994, he served as president of the Federal Reserve Bank of Boston. From 1986 to 1989, he was president of the Federal Home Loan Bank of Boston. Earlier, he served as Assistant to then Federal Reserve Chairman Paul Volcker, and as Deputy Assistant Secretary of the U.S. Treasury Department in Washington, D.C.

Mr. Syron was heavily involved in working through the banking crises in New England in the early 1990s. He was Chairman of the Boston College Board of Trustees and currently serves as a member of the boards of directors of John Hancock Mutual Life Insurance Company, Thermo Electron Corporation, and the Dreyfus Corporation.

Mr. Syron received a Ph.D. in economics from Tufts University in 1971 and an M.A. in the same field from Tufts two years earlier. A magna cum laude graduate of Boston College with a B.S. in economics, he holds honorary degrees from Boston College and Bentley College. Mr. Syron is married and has two children.

Laura Simone Unger. On February 12, 2001, President Bush designated Laura S. Unger Acting Chairman of the U.S. Securities and Exchange Commission. Ms. Unger was originally sworn in on November 5th, 1997 as a member of the U.S. Securities and Exchange Commission, for a term expiring June 2001.

Ms. Unger's main focus is the impact of technology on the securities industry. She is evaluating how the Commission can optimize the benefits of technology for the capital markets and investors, and has been working to implement recommendations made in her 1999 report to the Commission: "Online Brokerage: Keeping Apace of Cyberspace."

Soon after arriving at the Commission, Ms. Unger conducted a top-to-bottom review of the Commission's Enforcement Division. Ms. Unger also played a key role in the Commission's efforts to deal with Year 2000 remediation efforts by both public reporting companies and Commission-regulated entities.

Before being appointed to the Commission, Ms. Unger served as Securities Counsel to the United States Senate Committee on Banking, Housing and Urban Affairs where she advised the Chairman, Senator Alfonse M. D'Amato. Prior to working on Capital Hill, Ms. Unger was an attorney with the Enforcement Division of the U. S. Securities and Exchange Commission in Washington, D.C.

Ms. Unger received a B.A. in Rhetoric from the University of California at Berkeley in 1983, and a J.D. from New York Law School in 1987.

Daniel G. Weaver is currently an Associate Professor of Finance in the Zicklin School of Business, Baruch College. He holds degrees in English literature (BA, Seton Hall University) and finance (MBA, Ph.D. Rutgers University).

Dan's research and teaching focus is on security design, security market structure, and Internet trading. He has over 15 published articles. Recent papers include an examination of late trade reporting on Nasdaq, the impact of the public disclosure of limit order books on liquidity, potential visibility gains as a reason for listing, and the impact of tick size on market quality. He has served as a consultant to the New York Stock Exchange, Toronto Stock Exchange, and the Securities Industry Association.

Dan has been widely quoted in newspapers across the country including the Wall Street Journal, New York Times, Washington Post, USA Today, Associated Press, Barron's, Securities Week, Traders, and the Los Angeles Times. He has appeared on CNN, CNBC, PBS, NPR, and local radio and television. He has testified before the House Commerce Committee on the subject of decimalization.

Donald E. Weeden is Manager of Clearwater Ventures and WEB Investors, both LLCs, whose business is investing in high tech and internet related private businesses.

Mr. Weeden was also managing partner of Weeden Capital Partners, an early stage venture investment partnership that was successfully terminated in 1997.

Mr. Weeden's other venture activities include being a founding investor in National Semiconductor Corporation, Cadence Design, and Quantum Health and an early stage investor in Instinet and Autex.

Mr. Weeden has served on the Board of National Semiconductor since 1962 and presently serves on seven private venture companies.

Mr. Weeden is Chairman of Weeden Securities Corp., the General Partner of Weeden & Co., L.P., member of the NYSE and the NASD.

Robert A. Wood is a Distinguished Professor of Finance at the University of Memphis. Professor Wood previously taught at Penn State University for 14 years and NYU for one year. His education includes a Ph.D. in Finance from the University of Pittsburgh, a Masters in Operations Research from Stanford

University, and a Bachelors in Economics from the University of Washington. He was a member of the Presidential Task Force on Market Mechanisms (The Brady Commission) which studied the market crash in 1987, and a founding member of the NASD Economic Advisory Board. Professor Wood is the founder and Executive Director of the Institute for the Study of Security Markets, a non-profit Educational Foundation that promotes securities markets research by providing transactions data to academic institutions. He has consulted for various stock exchanges and investment firms around the world.

Prior to becoming an academic, Professor Wood held various positions in industry over a fifteen-year period.

John C. Woodman

Nottingham University, Industrial Economics: graduated 1976 Chartered Accountant: qualified 1979.

Member of Institute of Chartered Accountant's of Scotland research committee 1989 to 1995.

Thomson McLintock & Co: 1976 to 1984.

UBS Warburg and predecessor companies: 1984 to date COO European Equity business 1989 to 1997. Head of client management team 1997 to date.

London stock exchange: Chairman of Domestic and International equity Rules Committee 1997 to date.

R. Steven Wunsch is President of AZX, Inc., a company formed to design, build, market and operate an electronic single price auction trading system.

Previously, Mr. Wunsch worked in the Financial Futures Department of Kidder, Peabody, where he was a Vice President responsible for the Department's institutional customer index futures and equity trading activities. Prior to joining Kidder, Peabody, he was a floor trader and broker on the Amex Commodities and New York Futures Exchanges.

Mr. Wunsch received a BA in English Literature in 1969 from Princeton University

Index